Against the Odds

Janine Bempechat

Against the Odds

How "At-Risk" Children Exceed Expectations

Jossey-Bass Publishers
San Francisco

Jossey-Bass books and products are available through most bookstores. To contact Jossey-Bass directly, call (888) 378-2537, fax to (800) 605-2665, or visit our website at www.josseybass.com.

Substantial discounts on bulk quantities of Jossey-Bass books are available to corporations, professional associations, and other organizations. For details and discount information, contact the special sales department at Jossey-Bass.

For sales outside the United States, please contact your local Simon & Schuster International Office.

 Manufactured in the United States of America on Lyons Falls Turin Book. This paper is acid-free and 100 percent totally chlorine-free.

Library of Congress Cataloging-in-Publication Data

Bempechat, Janine, 1956–
    Against the odds : how "at-risk" students exceed expectations /
Janine Bempechat. — 1st ed.
        p. cm.
    Includes bibliographical references and index.
    ISBN 0-7879-4385-1 (cloth)
    1. Socially handicapped children—Education
(Elementary)—Massachusetts. 2. Minority children—Education
(Elementary)—Massachusetts. 3. Academic
achievement—Massachusetts. 4. Catholic schools   Massachusetts.
5. Public schools—Massachusetts. I. Title.
    LC4092.M4 B46 1998
    372.1826'94'09744—ddc21
                                                98-25348
                                                    CIP

FIRST EDITION
HB Printing   10 9 8 7 6 5 4 3 2 1

Contents

· ·

For my mother and father,
who started their lives over at midlife,
and taught us the importance of sacrifice and
persistence in the face of hardship.

Preface

This book describes the results of an ongoing research project that has taken the better part of six years to come to fruition. In my work, I have devoted my efforts to understanding poor and minority children who are successful in school, a constituency that has been long overlooked in scholarly research on academic achievement. I am part of a small but growing number of educational researchers who have begun to challenge common assumptions about poor families and schooling and to question accepted theories about how children's motivation contributes to their success or failure in school.

The reader may wonder why I have put quotations around the term "at-risk" in the subtitle of this book. This is because the students I focus on in this book fall into one or more categories of risk, such as poverty, low parent education, or ethnic and language minority status (Nakkula & Ravitch, 1998). However, these students are not failing, and they remain positive about learning and school.

As you will see, my methods are experimental and survey based, and they have been the vehicles with which I have broken new ground and gained new knowledge. One unintended effect of my work is that I do not like it anymore—not the topic, but the methods. And so a principal goal of this book is to convey my belief that a deeper conceptual understanding of achievement and motivation in poor and minority children is as yet beyond our reach, and will come only to the extent that we embrace methods that are more authentic and true to life—that is, in-depth, open-ended interviewing and ethnography.

I was trained in traditional developmental psychology and education, in which objectivity is considered the cornerstone of acceptable research practice. Along with my peers at McGill University and the Harvard Graduate School of Education, I was socialized in a research tradition that emphasized the importance of distancing ourselves from our own individual contexts so as not to taint our interpretations of research findings.

Given the intellectual tenor of our field at the time (the late seventies through the mid-eighties), I am not surprised that this is how I and my peers were prepared for the rigors of academic research. However, I am astonished that it has taken me so long to realize that we cannot and indeed should not separate ourselves from our contexts, whether we are analyzing interviews or testing statistical models. I am a very strong believer in the notion that, as researchers, we tend to take a keen interest in matters close to our hearts. Having been raised by Jewish immigrant parents who started their lives over at midlife, this has meant a curiosity about how parents get their children to do well in school. In the language of developmental psychology, I am interested in the influence of culture, ethnicity, and immigration on the socialization of achievement.

In early 1957, at the height of the Suez crisis, my parents fled Egypt—infant and preschooler in tow—leaving all things material behind. Their struggles for survival and upward mobility, characteristic of the many refugees who preceded and followed them, had a profound influence on how I came to understand the meaning of education and its relation to the future. I like to tell my students that in my family, there was God and there was the Teacher (in that order of priority), and as children, we could criticize neither. It was a given that we would do well in school; we had no other option— no relatives to fall back on for financial support, no inheritance in the offing. Despite the blatant anti-Semitism of President Nasser's

Egypt and Mayor Drapeau's Montreal, my parents maintained an unwavering belief that education would ensure us a good life.

Over time and after many opportunities to speak with high-achieving children of different ethnic and cultural backgrounds, I came to see that the messages my parents communicated—subtle and "mushy" as they were—were not unique. When I asked high-achieving Latino, Indochinese, African American, and Korean students to talk to me about their homes and how they were organized around issues of education, many conveyed the same parental beliefs and behaviors that I myself had experienced. Indeed, they could have been speaking of my own mother and father.

Thus emerged the overarching question that has guided the work presented in this book: What goes on in homes where children are doing well in school that may not be going on in homes where children are doing poorly? Are there factors related to school success that are culturally universal? To what extent, and how, might high achievers across ethnic groups resemble one another in their beliefs about learning and their perceptions of their parents' child-rearing practices, especially as these relate to education? And what influence might these common elements have on their school achievement? If culturally universal aspects of parental educational socialization foster success, surely there must also be aspects that are culturally specific. What are these? And how are they related to academic achievement?

With this book, I have come full circle. The work described here is a first step in expressing my interest in families and schooling. My methods are decontextualized by definition. In other words, my reliance on questionnaires and surveys has not allowed me to probe meaningfully the day-to-day lives of the students I have studied. I have moved on to a continued period of study, in which I give priority to the voices of the children and parents whose experiences I have sought to understand. Given my context—and despite what I know to be distressingly true of our society—I place my faith squarely in education, and I can only believe what my parents believed: that education is the only salvation in a society that may look down on you because of your religion, your ethnic background, or the color of your skin. Narrow-minded individuals will think what they may, but no one can take away your skills and credentials. It is thus that I embrace the view that all children can learn, that all parents can foster a love and respect for learning, and that all teachers can guide parents and children toward the fulfillment of intellectual potential.

OVERVIEW OF THE BOOK

With Chapter One, I examine the persistent and vexing problem of underachievement and the ways in which educational researchers have attempted to study school achievement in poor and minority students. I note that after decades of research we know far more about the factors that contribute to failure than about those that foster success. I argue that this distressing reality is largely due to the failure of educational researchers to integrate new knowledge about children's motivation to succeed in school with an understanding of the cultures and contexts in which their learning takes place. Having stated the problem, I provide the background to my studies, including information about the participating schools and children and the questionnaires I used to gather information.

In Chapter Two, I provide the context in which previous research on achievement in low-income students has taken place. In particular, I chronicle how educational researchers and policymakers came to change their thinking about poor families. Whereas families in poverty were viewed as entities that needed to be "fixed" to resemble middle-class families, researchers and policymakers now demonstrate far more respect for the strengths that all parents have as they cope with raising their children under trying circumstances. I also present a synopsis of my research findings and demonstrate the degree to which commonly held views about academic achievement in low-income students are unfounded.

I present the findings from my various research studies separately according to each of the main themes I investigated. Readers interested in details related to measures and data analysis can refer to my published work, a listing of which appears in the Suggestions for Further Reading section at the back of the book. Thus, Chapter Three focuses on how students are socialized for schooling and learning. I examine how students perceive their parents' child-rearing practices as they relate to education, with a particular emphasis on the ways in which culture and ethnicity may guide both the beliefs about schooling that parents' convey to their children and the ways in which parents may structure their homes to encourage academic achievement.

In Chapter Four, I examine ethnic differences and similarities in students' beliefs about the causes of success and failure in school in general, and in mathematics in particular. In addition to comparing the beliefs of students across the different ethnic groups, I also compare the beliefs of all high-achieving students, regardless of ethnic group. This allows me to draw important inferences about aspects of achievement beliefs that may be universal.

Chapter Five describes what I have learned about mathematics achievement, how it is differentially associated with children's perceptions of their parents' child-rearing practices, and their assessments of the reasons for success and failure. I demonstrate that, across ethnic groups, high achievers are remarkably similar to one another in their perceptions of their parents' educational beliefs and practices, and I provide evidence countering the commonly accepted view that high achievement is directly related to beliefs in the value of effort.

In Chapter Six, I weave together our findings into a compelling story about high achievement in the lives of poor and minority students and follow this in Chapter Seven with a pragmatic discussion of how our results can help parents and teachers think about fostering achievement in the lives of their children and students.

Finally, in Chapter Eight I step back to take a critical look at what I have contributed to our understanding of the phenomenon of academic success in poor and minority children. In thinking about the various ways in which our field can direct itself, I will argue that "less is more"—that we will gain a deeper conceptual understanding of academic achievement in low-income students by spending more time with smaller numbers of children and parents. As researchers, we must make a greater effort to focus on the ways in which cultural notions of ourselves and the society in which we live are organized and operate in the daily lives of children and their parents (Shweder, 1990). Researchers and practitioners have struggled for a very long time to understand the enigma of achievement and motivation in ethnic America. I will argue that the complexities with which we have struggled will smooth themselves out when we make a concerted effort to combine more meaningful ways of studying education in children's lives with the more traditional large-scale surveys of children's and parents' attitudes about learning.

Acknowledgments

· ·

This book would not have been possible without the participation of the many parents, children, and teachers who graciously gave of their time so that I could better understand education in their lives. I am grateful for the continued support of Sister Ann Dominic Roach, superintendent of schools of the Catholic Archdiocese in Boston, and Sister Kathleen Carr, its director of external relations, as well as the many administrators and teachers at schools in and around Boston. The work reported here was supported generously by the Spencer Foundation, the National Science Foundation, and the Harvard Graduate School of Education's Faculty Research Funding awards.

I owe a great debt of gratitude to my teachers and colleagues who have supported my research since the late 1980s. I owe this book to Bob LeVine, who convinced me that it was time to tell this story, and to Susan Holloway, who guided me through the daunting first experience of crafting a book prospectus.

I am very fortunate to have the continued support of my senior colleagues at the Harvard Graduate School of Education. Howard Gardner, Kurt Fischer, Bob Selman, Catherine Snow, and John Willett devoted time in their extremely busy lives to provide me with valuable feedback on different parts of the manuscript. Mike Nakkula and Suzanne Graham, friends and collaborators, provided substantive insights into what the data were telling us.

I have been blessed to count Herb Ginsburg at Teachers College, Columbia University, and Thalma Lobel at the University of Tel Aviv as supportive and enthusiastic teachers, collaborators, and mentors since my graduate school days.

I am indebted to Salie Abrahams of the University of the Western Cape, who encouraged me to encounter theories in the context of my own experiences and taught me that we learn nothing from worshiping either theory or theorist, and to Ellie Drago-Severson, who, with grace and patience, taught me about the values of qualitative research. Friends and collaborators both, they have contributed much to my understanding of the importance of meaning making in children's lives.

I owe a special debt of gratitude to John Nicholls, with whom I never had the honor to study, but who nonetheless showed a keen interest in my work since my professional beginnings. When I was still a graduate student, John came to my first poster display at the 1985 conference of the Society for Research in Child Development, read it with care, and offered thoughtful feedback. He came by every poster I presented in subsequent years to comment on my thinking and my progress. I don't think he ever realized how much his generosity and kind support meant to me over the years, and his untimely passing is a loss for all of us who care about children and learning.

Over the years, my students have worked and argued with me and ultimately helped my thinking about poor families evolve. I thank the good fortune that brought Norma Jimenez from L.A.'s sun to Boston's winters. She constantly engages me in discussions of Talmudic proportions, and her influence on my thinking is reflected in these pages. I owe a great thanks also to Gisell Quihuis, Jennifer Ekert, Jin Li, Mia Omori Yamada, and John Wu for their critiques and insights.

I am grateful for the thoughtful feedback provided to me by Mark Springer, principal, and first-grade teacher Tom Daniels of the Mason-Rice School in Newton Centre, as well as my good friends

Amy Cooper and Leslie Anderson, all of whom who helped me learn to write in language that is accessible to teachers and parents.

At Jossey-Bass, Leslie Berriman's good nature and patient teaching never wavered during the process of turning my ideas into a manuscript. All I have done in this volume has been strengthened by her wisdom.

I am indebted to Cathy Bracken, Ally Raabe, Jason LaPointe, and Ellen Slotnick at Seattle's Best Coffee in Newton Centre, who graciously provided me with the warm and welcoming workplace where much of this book was written.

I thank Tracey Doherty, whose love and good humor kept our family going in so many ways while I was preoccupied with this work. Finally, I express my love and thankfulness to my children, Becca and Adam, who patiently tolerated my absences while I completed my "chapter" book, and to my husband, David, for his love and unwavering belief in me.

Against the Odds

Introduction:
Learning from Poor and Minority
Students Who Succeed

*My parents immigrated to the United States from
Mexico when I was just four years old. They worked
so hard—extremely hard—and so did we because that
was the only way we knew we were going to make it.
My Mom got a paper route, and we all helped out,
getting up at four in the morning to help deliver the
papers. After the paper route was done, my Mom got
us ready for school and went off to spend the day
cleaning houses. My Dad worked on an assembly line
during the day, part time at a gasoline station in the
afternoons, and at a pizza factory at night. They
helped the four of us get through college and graduate
school, not with monetary support, but by demonstrating persistence.*

Raymond's story is a story of success—of sacrifices made by parents for the long-term benefit of their children's futures. It
could not have been easy to uproot themselves and their children,
to leave all that was familiar and move to Los Angeles—a city whose
open dislike of Chicanos had done little to promote itself as friendly
to migrating Mexican families such as Raymond's. Yet Raymond's
family did indeed migrate, eyes wide open to the discrimination

they would likely face, and they never looked back. As far as they were concerned, they did right by their children.

This is one family's story of success against the odds, a story that is replayed in the lives of many families. The willingness to sacrifice for the sake of children's futures is a characteristic of all families, rich and poor, majority and minority. Raymond and his siblings stand apart from their peers, however, because they are successfully navigating the journey from working-class to middle-class status. What is it about Raymond, his siblings, and his parents that has enabled them to succeed where so many others falter? This is the question that I attempt to answer in this book.

All of us, parents, teachers, researchers, and public policymakers alike, continue to be greatly concerned about the education of children like Raymond, particularly in light of the fact that the proportion of poor and minority children in schools is expected to increase dramatically as we move into the next century. For those of us who are committed to bettering educational opportunities for poor and minority students, it has been very troubling to know that, barring serious learning difficulties or mental retardation, all young children have the basic intellectual skills and the potential to learn, yet many poor and minority children are failing to reach their intellectual potential.

While this overall picture may be discouraging, we do know that some poor and minority children excel in school. Why is this? Unfortunately, we know surprisingly little about the factors that contribute to their high achievement. Our limited knowledge comes largely from three kinds of studies. In the first type, which educational researchers refer to as *retrospective* studies, successful adults bring their perspectives from the present to bear on their recollections of critical influences in their past. For example, Charles Harrington and his colleagues (Harrington & Boardman, 1997) have found that successful adults who were reared in poverty speak extensively of the importance of a caring adult, or mentor, in their lives—a parent, teacher, or some member of their extended family who had faith in their academic potential and encouraged them, through word and deed, to pursue their education to the fullest.

A second kind of educational research, which is called *ethnographic*, consists of studies in which educational researchers interview family members at length and observe their daily lives. Reginald Clark's (1983) study of twenty African American families, all of whom were poor and living in the same housing development, is a prime example of this kind of work. Clark's observations and interviews were centered on understanding the differences between the ten families where children were excelling in school and the remaining families, where children were behind in their schoolwork and failing.

A third kind of research consists of *large-scale surveys* of children and their parents. These kinds of studies typically probe a wide variety of factors related to homes and schools that are relevant for children's academic performance. For example, survey studies have found that poor and minority teenagers in Catholic high schools fare much better than their peers who attend public high schools. Specifically, they attain higher grade point averages (GPAs) and higher Scholastic Achievement Test (SAT) scores, and also graduate from high school and attend college at much higher rates (Bryk, Lee, & Holland, 1993).

Studies of minority student achievement that have resulted from these three kinds of research streams have been helpful in illuminating specific factors that have an influence on school performance, such as high expectations on the part of parents, or the availability of higher-level courses in a school's curriculum. I believe that two major shortcomings in these research studies have limited our ability to understand the dynamics of high achievement in students ordinarily considered to be at risk for school failure. First is the fact that this research has been conducted independent of important advances that have taken place in the field of achievement motivation. Educational researchers who study children's motivation to succeed in school have made a great deal of progress in understanding how children's beliefs about school achievement influence their learning styles. For example, children who believe that intelligence is a quality that grows without limits tend to seek and embrace challenging assignments in the classroom. In contrast, those who view intelligence as a quality that is finite in nature tend to avoid challenging assignments for fear of making mistakes (Bempechat, London, & Dweck, 1991; Dweck & Bempechat, 1983). This raises the question of whether high-achieving minority students are those who might believe their intelligence to be malleable and unlimited, but existing studies do not address that point.

Second, with the exception of a few ethnographic studies, the vast majority of the research I have discussed has failed to consider the critical importance of children's cultures and the contexts in which their parents are raising them. The findings of survey studies, for example, would be much more powerful and useful to educators if they included information that helped teachers understand how different cultures and contexts guide and influence parents' beliefs about how they should raise their children. The result is that we lack a comprehensive understanding of what makes some students excel where so many others falter.

We are at a crossroads. The truth is that after decades of proposing theoretical models and implementing intervention programs in schools, we know far more about the factors that foster underachievement and school failure than those that contribute to academic success in poor and minority children. This is not to say that underachievement is a trivial concern. Nonetheless, it is distressing that, after so much time, money, and effort have been spent, high achievement among poor and minority children continues to be a little-understood phenomenon.

WHY STUDY SUCCESS?

It may seem counterintuitive to express concern over children who are doing well in school. Why bother? These children have demonstrated that they are flourishing and probably will continue to flourish academically, whether they attend a parochial Catholic or a neighborhood public school. I believe that this view is shortsighted and misses the point entirely. In fact, our anxieties over school failure should be driving our efforts to understand success. At this time in our social history, there is mounting concern over underachievement in general (especially in mathematics and science), and minority underachievement in particular. With globalization has come a greater dependence on technologically relevant skills, and all of us—parents, researchers, educators, and public policymakers—agree that we can ill afford to see our children's intellectual competence increasingly at risk. It stands to reason then, that we will learn a great deal about promoting school success by studying those students who seem to defy the odds.

Further, as the population of students becomes increasingly ethnic, we have an obligation as educational researchers to understand how academic achievement is influenced by culture and ethnicity. We cannot assume that particular elements of home and school that foster school achievement in one group will have the same effect on other groups. Nor, for that matter, can we afford the luxury of assuming that there is but one successful pattern of child rearing in any one group. In other words, we must at the same time confront the issues that inevitably arise when we attempt to draw comparisons between ethnic groups and among members of any one group in particular.

Surprisingly, we know almost nothing about how high-achieving students across ethnic groups might resemble or differ from one another. Is high achievement a culturally universal phenomenon? That is, regardless of ethnic group, are there aspects of student beliefs and parental child-rearing practices that foster high achievement? Or are there culturally specific aspects of beliefs and child rearing that lead to success in different ethnic groups? Or might some combination of both lead to academic success?

In addition, the generally monolithic approach to the study of ethnicity and achievement has deprived teachers and researchers of the opportunity to understand what might distinguish high from low achievers *within* a particular ethnic group. For example, while it is helpful to know that Indochinese students tend to exceed the academic accomplishments of all other ethnic groups, it is equally helpful—if not more so—to know the ways in which high- and low-achieving Indochinese students might differ from one another. As Drago-Severson (Bempechat & Drago-Severson, 1998) has suggested, this knowledge would allow us to move beyond ethnic stereotypes, which can have such a devastating effect on children's self-esteem and academic achievement. In the case of Indochinese and other students of Asian descent, the unspoken expectation on the part of teachers that they all excel in school places enormous pressure on students to do well. I am hard-pressed to decide who is worse off—those who meet or those who fall short of such expectations. The former experience seemingly unrelentingly high expectations for their school performance; the latter are met with astonished disappointment. Imagine the recollected experience of Lisa, a graduate student of Chinese descent: "The first days of school, I could see a wave of relief wash over my teachers' faces. It was as if, when they saw me, they were saying to themselves, 'Oh, thank goodness, at least there's one student I don't have to worry about.'"

Educational researchers who study the academic experiences of students like Lisa have come to refer to these stereotyped expectations as the myth of the "model minority" (Sue & Okazaki, 1990; see Liu, 1998). They have argued very forcefully that there are a great many students of Asian descent who are not models of academic excellence and that their ethnic group is not a model minority, better than or above other minority groups. I believe very strongly that if educational researchers work to understand the experiences of high and low achievers *within* ethnic groups, they will be able to provide teachers with practical advice that can help them help all children reach their intellectual potential.

Clearly, the many issues involved in understanding school success are not easy ones for any teacher, researcher, or public policymaker to contend with. It should come as no surprise, then, that there is little consensus over the ways in which we should go about increasing our understanding of academic excellence. In this book, I argue that if we are to make genuine progress, the field of educational research must embrace notions commonly accepted in cultural psychology. First, child development is embedded in culture and context. It is simply not possible to understand how ethnic minority children grow and develop, both socially and academically, without first understanding how different cultures and social contexts influence the ways in which people come to understand the world around them. Second, parents and teachers are the agents of their culture—the ones who transmit cultural beliefs and practices to children. This implies that they are guided in their socialization practices by the very cultures in which they live. Third, to deepen our understanding of issues as complex as children's motivation to succeed in school, we must undertake serious consideration of what psychologists refer to as "meaning making in context." This means that we must pay very close attention to how children and parents shape their understanding of schooling and education in their own contexts. We must give greater importance to the language that parents and children use to describe their experiences with schooling, the perspectives they bring to bear on their experiences, and the beliefs that develop as a result of these experiences (Schurmans & Dasen, 1992). Educational researchers who incorporate these views will undoubtedly provide teachers with information that is genuinely helpful for their daily work.

BEHIND THE STUDIES

By 1990, I had completed enough research on the school achievement of Cambodian refugee children to pique my interest in the phenomenon of high achievement in general. As I mentioned in the Preface, it seemed to me that many of the home experiences that these children relayed to me were ones that could have easily described my own background and upbringing. Clearly, while the historical circumstances differed, these children and I had in common our families' experience of immigration to a new and completely different culture. I realized, however, that there was something more involved than the immigrant experience. These students and I came from completely different backgrounds and cultures, yet there they sat, saying things about their parents and their homes that I could have said about my own parents, my own home. At times they seemed to be describing my own mother and father, particularly when they spoke of their parents' reverence for the teacher and the ways in which their home lives seemed to revolve around their schoolwork. At the same time, they depicted aspects of their parents' child-rearing practices that were very different from those of my parents. And so began the formulation of the questions I have been pursuing since 1990—are there universal aspects of child rearing and socialization that contribute to academic achievement? If these high-achieving Cambodian children and I could relay similar descriptions of our parents' views on schooling, would high-achieving African American and Latino students convey similar depictions of their parents?

What about cultural differences? It only makes sense that students from different ethnic backgrounds would identify child-rearing practices that would be specific to their own cultures. What would be these differences? In other words, how might child-rearing practices meant to promote academic achievement differ between parents of different ethnic groups?

I began the Harvard Study of Schooling in the fall of 1990. Given my interest in poor and minority students, I sought and received permission to work with several public and Catholic school districts that draw on poor communities for their student populations. These included areas in the cities of Boston, Lowell, and Lynn, Massachusetts. I focused exclusively on children in the later elementary school grades—fifth and sixth—for a specific and theoretically justified reason. Researchers who have studied children's motivation to achieve have consistently found that it is in the period between fifth and sixth grade that their beliefs about their intellectual abilities seem to gel, so to speak, and become stable (Nicholls, 1989). From this point on, children's judgment of their abilities and their beliefs about the reasons for success and failure do not tend to vary on a short-term basis. In contrast, children from preschool through the fourth grade seem to change their beliefs about learning more frequently.

My decision to compare public and Catholic school students was not random. By the time I began my research, it had become increasingly apparent that children ordinarily considered to be at risk for school failure were flourishing in Catholic schools, and I wanted to understand how their motivation to achieve might differ from that of their public school peers. I learned quickly that there had been a long-brewing controversy surrounding educational research that aimed to compare the school achievement of public with Catholic school students. Simply put, this scholarly dispute concerned the issue of parental choice. It is entirely conceivable that poor and minority students do better in Catholic than in public schools *because they are better students to begin with*. This line of reasoning argues that parents who make the conscious choice to send their children to Catholic schools may differ in very important ways from parents who do not make this choice. It is possible, for example, that relative to parents who stay with public schooling, those who select Catholic schooling may be more concerned about and involved in their children's education, and their children may themselves be more motivated to learn and excel in school. In other words, the population of Catholic school students is a *self-selected* one, and any comparisons to a population of students that has not consciously selected an alternative to public schooling is inappropriate.

While there is some merit to this argument, I chose to enter the research fray because I believe that the changing demographics of the childhood population make it increasingly possible to disentangle the effects of self-selection from the positive influences of Catholic schooling. That is to say, where Catholic schools may have once tested for and recruited the cream of the academic crop, they now find themselves in competition with public schools for a dwindling pool of children. Parish schools now wage marketing campaigns to bring students into their schools. To my mind, something very important is going on in Catholic schools that is contributing to the academic success that is being enjoyed by poor and minority children. I believe very strongly that educational researchers have an obligation to better understand what this "something" is.

My attempt to understand this led me to focus on two areas of influence. My first focus was the family, where so much early structuring of learning takes place. How do parents encourage academic achievement? What kinds of things do they say to their children about the importance of schooling, and what kinds of things do they do to create a home environment that is supportive of intellectual pursuits? My second focus was the children themselves, more specifically, their beliefs about the causes of success and failure in mathematics. When children judge their performance in school, to what extent do they credit their performance to factors such as innate ability or effort or to external influences such as luck? As I will show later on, each of these explanations has a different influence on whether children will choose challenging assignments and persist in the face of difficulty or challenge.

To answer these questions, I used an original questionnaire of students' perceptions of their parents' involvement in their schooling, as well as a well-regarded questionnaire of children's reasons for success and failure in mathematics. I also asked the students to complete a widely used ten-minute timed test of mathematics computation. I must underscore that the work presented in this book did not include interviews with parents about their attitudes about their children's schooling or their strategies for encouraging success in school. Throughout this book, when I speak of such strategies, I am referring to the *children's* perceptions of their parents' child-rearing practices and attitudes about schooling. I make no claims whatsoever about what may actually be occurring to foster or inhibit academic achievement in these children's homes. Additionally, the measure of mathematics achievement in my research—the Wide Range Achievement Test (WRAT)—is a widely used, relatively straightforward test of computational skills. I make no claims about other types of mathematics achievement, such as abstract or logical thinking skills. It is important for the reader to understand these caveats in order to have a basis for evaluating the work I present in this book. Having stated these clearly, I move on in the next chapter to examine how the national discourse on poor families has evolved over the past few decades. I will argue that our continued inability to understand high achievement in poor and minority students is due largely to a failure in educational research to take into account theoretical advances that have been made in children's motivation to succeed in school and to incorporate these advances into our understanding of parents' influences in their children's schooling. The past two decades have been witness to the development of a much deeper, conceptual understanding of the powerful influence that children's own beliefs about learning and schooling can have on their actual school performance. Educational researchers who wish to help teachers help their students succeed must begin to examine how parents influence the development of their children's attitudes about schooling and learning.

In addition, I contend that our ability to understand how "at-risk" children exceed expectations will remain limited as long as educational researchers overlook the critical contributions that have been made by scholars who study the cultures and contexts in which learning takes place. Attitudes about schooling vary considerably as a function of parents' ethnic and cultural backgrounds, and these attitudes need to be taken into account in any study of children's motivation to achieve in school.

2

Misguided Notions
About Underachievement

The latter half of this century has witnessed an important shift in how researchers, educators, and policymakers understand the persistent puzzle of underachievement among poor and minority children. There was a time when the poor performance of low-income children was blamed openly on their parents. Clearly, something must have been terribly awry in the homes of families living in poverty. The prevailing view was that, in all likelihood, poor children suffered from many deficiencies at home, the most critical of which was lack of intellectual stimulation. This focus on deficits within families gradually gave way to a more complex understanding that acknowledged the many influences in children's school achievement, including parents, teachers, school environment, and community surroundings. Furthermore, it has become increasingly clear that family poverty does not necessarily imply family dysfunction. Indeed, all families, poor and rich, have strengths and weaknesses. Educators and researchers alike have realized that they can have much more impact on the problem of underachievement if they search for solutions in the strengths that lie within families.

Despite this move from family deficits to family strengths, our ability to appreciate high achievement in poor and minority students has been limited, largely because educational researchers have not linked current knowledge about children's motivation in school with new insights into the critical role that parents play in socializing their children to be students. This oversight has been compounded further by a general tendency to neglect the contexts and cultures in which children are raised. After all, it only makes sense that whatever it is that educational researchers have learned about children's motivation and parents' influences must vary as a function of the cultures in which children grow.

In this chapter, I present a brief synopsis of my research findings, and I demonstrate how several commonly held views about academic achievement in low-income students are actually quite unfounded.

THE EVOLUTION OF OUR KNOWLEDGE

Research on achievement in low-income children has matured. Not long ago, researchers operated under two connected and damaging premises. The first was a theoretical approach to educational research that viewed underachievement as the result of lack of cognitive stimulation in the home and the school (for example, Hess & Shipman, 1965). The second was an enduring public policy position that perceived poor families as dysfunctional and in need of major intervention that would "save" them, or at the very least, "fix" what was wrong with them (Glazer & Moynihan, 1963).

Indeed, when efforts at compensatory education began in earnest in the 1960s with national intervention programs such as Head Start, the prevailing attitude was that low-income parents failed to provide their children with adequate stimulation and training, thus stunting their basic cognitive development. This was seen as the primary cause of school failure (Ginsburg, Bempechat, & Chung, 1992). Educational researchers firmly believed that intervention efforts would pay off; with time, poor families would surely come to resemble white middle-class families in their structure and child-rearing practices (Ginsburg, 1972, 1986). At the time, the notion that white middle-class families were exemplars of well-functioning families did not seem to warrant further scrutiny. Scholarship on the dynamics of family functioning has clearly demonstrated that family pathology does not discriminate. That is to say, financial security, in and of itself, is not an inoculation against family dysfunction.

There is no question that educational researchers engaged in a fair bit of finger pointing, aimed squarely at poor mothers and fathers. This kind of arrogant thinking has thankfully given way to a more sophisticated view of families as systems that exist in the context of larger communities. And indeed, this "deficit model" was very much a product of its time. With President Johnson's declared War on Poverty, the prevailing view was that if the government threw enough money at the problem of family pathology, it would gradually resolve itself. That this intervention did not have the intended positive effects is reflective of the naïveté of scholars and politicians who, while not unaware of the complex task before them, failed to consider the degree to which culture, context, and motivation each play critical and unique roles in preparing children to enter school with positive attitudes and high expectations for success.

In fact, any intervention or policy whose goal is to save individuals is bound to fail, for in the very act of saving, we communicate our belief that those whom we perceive to be in need are incapable of problem solving and limited in their abilities to save themselves. As Bernard Weiner (1994) has argued, this has a tendency to foster feelings of incompetence, which may lead to learned helplessness—quite the opposite of what well-intentioned academics and policymakers had conceived.

For the most part, our understandings from this period in our social history have evolved. The deficit model fell into disfavor as educational research accumulated to reveal that most poor children do not suffer deficits in basic cognitive functioning. Researchers now know, for example, that there are no differences between low- and middle-income children in early thinking about mathematics.

Scholars such as Herbert Ginsburg (1997) have urged educational researchers to eschew the position that any deficits originating within the family are the *cause* of poor performance. As Aaron Pallas and his colleagues have pointed out (Pallas, Natriello, & McDill, 1989), an otherwise strong family may not have the skills to provide its children with positive educational experiences. This does *not* imply that family members cannot *acquire* these skills.

Where underachievement was once viewed as resulting from deficient homes or inefficient schools, we now acknowledge that the responsibility for our children's education is a mutual one, shared by the home, the school, and the community. This means that no one individual is to blame for the fact that a particular child may not be reaching his or her intellectual potential; that no one group of individuals is to blame for a given school's low showing on districtwide tests. On the contrary, I believe that a child's success—and a school's success—is very much an indication of the commitment of family members, schoolteachers and administrators, and community leaders.

In this regard, Joyce Epstein and James Comer have written eloquently about the necessity of home-school-community partnerships in ensuring children's academic achievement (Comer, 1980; Epstein, 1987). Educational research now speaks of the importance of understanding the strengths that lie within families and capitalizing on these strengths, and of appreciating the positive consequences that come from nurturing a sense of efficacy and empowerment in family members. This paradigm shift is nontrivial, in that it has oriented researchers and practitioners toward the study of success. Where academic achievement is concerned, our collective knowledge has been advanced by a variety of research programs that have adopted different methods of inquiry. This commitment to multiple methods has yielded new insights, but attempts to integrate these into a coherent story of success against the odds have been limited.

WHAT HAVE WE LEARNED, AND
HOW HAVE WE LEARNED IT?

As noted in Chapter One, three primary classes of educational research have provided the bulk of information that we have about the paths to success for poor and minority children: retrospective studies, ethnographic studies, and large-scale surveys of children and their parents.

Retrospective studies often highlight the importance of mentoring. For example, Charles Harrington and his colleagues (Boardman, Harrington, & Horowitz, 1987) describe how one African American woman, a partner in a prestigious law firm, spoke of a college professor who, when he learned that she wanted to go to law school but did not think she could get in, drove her several hundred miles to the school that became her alma mater. He helped her complete her application and rejoiced with her when she was admitted.

Reginald Clark's ethnographic study (1983) of twenty African American families living in the same housing development found that the children who were doing well in school came from homes that were very structured. In these homes the parents' expectations for their children's social behavior and school achievement were very clearly stated, and the children knew the consequences that would result from transgressions of any kind. These were homes in which parents were very familiar with their children's schools; they knew their children's teachers and were aware of what and when homework assignments were due and when tests were to take place. Clark characterized these parents as being firm but warm in their child-rearing styles.

In contrast, Clark noted that children who were failing in school came from homes that were very disorganized, even chaotic. There were no clearly articulated rules or expectations for either the children's behavior or their academic performance. These parents tended to be out of the loop, so to speak, with regard to their children's schools. That is, they often did not know the names of their children's teachers, were unsure of what their children were being taught, and did not know if and when their children had homework to complete or tests to study for. Clark described these parents as being rather permissive in their child-rearing styles. Large-scale surveys typically probe a variety of school, home, and social factors that have been identified as predictors of success in poor students (e.g., Luster & McAdoo, 1994; Peng & Wright, 1994). These include demanding curricula, high parental expectations, and peer support for learning (Fordham & Ogbu, 1986; Hilton, Hsia, Solorzano, & Benton, 1989; Scott-Jones, 1987). For example, Hilton et al. (1989) studied factors that predicted persistence in science among high-achieving minority students. They found that the availability of and enrollment in advanced courses, as well as participation in math clubs and teams, were strongly associated with high achievement and continued persistence in science-related studies.

While this research has been invaluable in spelling out factors that are influential in the school achievement of poor children, the field of educational research lacks a theoretically grounded view of what makes some children excel where so many others fall behind. We simply do not have an overall understanding of success against the odds that is based in an explanatory theory. As noted earlier, very little of the existing research has taken advantage of advances that have been made in theories of children's motivation to succeed in school. Even less of this work has focused on weaving together findings that result from more traditional quantitative studies with those from less common qualitative studies.

For example, many surveys have reported that parent involvement is a critical component of children's success in school (Epstein, 1987). It would be very interesting to know how parents describe their roles, the kinds of involvement that teachers find useful as well as the kinds they find offensive, and how children interpret the different ways that their parents involve themselves in schoolwork.

Information of this nature would tell an interesting story that would complement nicely the knowledge that has been gained from surveys that researchers have conducted. Further, the attempt to seek this information from ethnic minority parents would fill a distressing void in educational research (Fisher, Jackson, & Villarruel, 1998). As I will argue later, we cannot possibly hope to be of real help to parents and teachers unless we work to understand their beliefs and perspectives as they articulate them.

WHY STUDY CHILDREN'S MOTIVATION?

There is a very important benefit to studying how high achievers are motivated. Over the past twenty-five years, educational researchers have learned that children have different ways of interpreting their experiences with success and failure in the classroom, and these different interpretations have a profound influence on how children come to view their intellectual abilities. Precisely how children come to see themselves as "smart" or "average" or "dumb," and the way these beliefs influence their willingness to take on challenging assignments and persist in the face of difficulty, has been the focus of much of the research in children's motivation. The primary goal underlying these research efforts is the belief that if we can learn how negative attitudes about learning develop, we may be able to halt the downward spiral in confidence and expectations that often results from feelings of intellectual inferiority.

It would not be unreasonable to think that brighter or "smarter" children have a leg up, so to speak—that better-than-average intelligence will propel children to excel in school and thus protect them from being done in by low confidence. In fact, it is more often the case that children's confidence and their beliefs about their abilities are better indicators of how well they will do in school than their actual IQ or achievement test scores (see Dweck &

Bempechat, 1983). This has very interesting implications. First, it means that there are very bright children who rarely seem to fulfill their intellectual potential, perhaps because they fear the mistakes that are often associated with challenging classroom assignments. At one time or another, surely all teachers have worked with children such as these. More important for teachers, however, is the implication that there are children who are not "smart" as defined by IQ tests but who nonetheless manage to do extremely well in the classroom, possibly because they are willing to take on challenging assignments, relatively unfettered by worries about the consequences of making mistakes. Quite simply, these children push themselves—and perhaps because of this they become "smarter" over time (in terms of practical success) than their more intelligent peers.

It is thus that current approaches to studying children's motivation in school are focused on the critical importance of a variety of beliefs that affect learning in the classroom, such as children's confidence in their abilities to learn something new or to successfully complete an assignment; their expectations for experiencing success or failure at the end of their efforts; the grades they would be satisfied with, or put another way, their personal standards for their performance in the classroom; their own judgments of how smart they think they are in different subjects; and how much effort they think they need to invest in an assignment in order to do well. All these kinds of beliefs about achievement influence the assignments that children choose to pursue and the persistence with which they pursue them (see Dweck & Bempechat, 1983).

Three related streams of inquiry, all centered on children's perceptions of their intellectual ability and the magnitude of the efforts they expend, are most relevant to the research project I present in this book. I describe these avenues of research in the following sections and show how they guided the design of my research on success against the odds.

Children's Beliefs About the Reasons for Success and Failure

My work was very much guided by an understanding that any study of children's school achievement would be incomplete without paying serious attention to children's beliefs about the causes of success and failure. My view was greatly influenced by the work of the noted scholar Bernard Weiner (1994), who has found that the reasons to which students ascribe their school performance, good or bad, actually predict how they will feel about their academic abilities, and these feelings or emotions predict how they will approach learning in the future—whether they avoid or embrace studying, for example.

Weiner has shown that, when asked to provide possible reasons to explain times when they succeed and times when they fail in school, students tend to focus on four primary causes. On any given occasion, students may cite one or more of these causes as having influenced their performance. The first of these is innate *ability* or intelligence, which many students acknowledge is an important factor in their academic success. The second is *effort*. Many students credit trying hard as a necessary component in school achievement. The third is the relative *ease* with which they believe they succeeded at the task. Finally, students will mention *external factors* that in all likelihood had nothing to do with their performance, such as having been lucky enough to study the right material or being the teacher's pet. As the reader may expect, students tend to attribute failure to the opposite causes: lack of the ability required to be successful at the assignment, failure to invest enough effort into the work, the high difficulty level of the task, and external factors such as bad luck on that day.

Weiner and many others who study children's beliefs have been able to demonstrate that when a student believes that he failed the math test because he is dumb in math, this will likely make him feel incompetent and unhappy about his math skills. Under these circumstances, he will probably not invest a great deal of effort in preparation for the next math test, on which his performance will likely stay the same or deteriorate. There really is no point, since, according to the vast majority of students, intelligence is a characteristic of individuals that resides within and is neither changeable nor within one's command. In other words, as Weiner has argued, *ability* is perceived as *internal*, *stable*, and *uncontrollable*.

In contrast, the student who believes that she failed the math test because she did not study hard or long enough will likely feel guilty, and these feelings of guilt will probably propel her to begin preparing well in advance of the next math test, on which her performance is likely to improve. According to Weiner, *effort* is a quality that resides within, and is both changeable and within one's command. In other words, it is an *internal*, *unstable*, and *controllable* factor in a student's learning.

Studies of children's reasoning about the causes of success and failure have served as the foundation for many strong research endeavors in children's motivation in school for several decades. One of these endeavors has been the study of children's beliefs about effort and ability. If children so readily invoke effort and ability (or lack of effort and lack of ability) to explain their performance in school, then what do they think about their efforts and their abilities? More specifically, how hard do they think they have to try in order to do well in school? How smart do they think they are? And how does their reasoning about effort and ability influence the assignments they choose to pursue and the persistence with which they pursue them?

Perceptions of Ability

I spoke earlier about different ways that children have of thinking about or judging their intellectual abilities. Two prominent educational researchers, John Nicholls and Carol Dweck, have written separately about how some children tend to believe that intelligence is a quality that can grow infinitely. These children will tend to agree with statements such as "As long as you learn new things, you can always get smarter and smarter" (Dweck & Bempechat, 1983). In contrast, other children tend more to the view that intelligence is a trait that is fixed from birth and that "You can learn new things, but how smart you are stays pretty much the same."

Of most relevance to teachers is the finding that children's choice of challenging or unchallenging assignments and the persistence they will demonstrate on a new assignment is different, depending on whether they believe intelligence to be unlimited or fixed. Specifically, children who view intelligence as a fluid and changeable quality will tend more toward undertaking challenging tasks, even when their confidence is low and they risk mistakes and failure. And when faced with difficulty or failure, they tend to rebound and behave as though they believe they have control over the situation, or that they are in command. They become persistent and absorbed with finding effective ways to strategize their way to a solution. Researchers have often found that these children talk out loud to themselves, saying things like "I know I should just concentrate more" or "I think I should retrace my steps." This kind of self-monitoring is very helpful in keeping children focused on the task at hand (Diener & Dweck, 1978, 1980). In addition, children who tend to believe in a flexible view of intelligence will also tend to describe intelligence in others on the basis of the actions they take to become smarter. They say things like "He's smart because he always does his homework" or "She's smart because she always tries her hardest" (Bempechat, et al., 1991). These children seem to be oriented toward the notion that learning is a process, one that allows them to increase both their skills and their knowledge. For children so oriented, worries about how "smart" they are relative to others do not figure prominently in their concerns about their schoolwork.

In contrast, children who believe in a fixed view of intelligence tend to choose easy over challenging assignments. These are precisely the kinds of tasks that allow them to show off their abilities with little or no fear of making mistakes. These children will actually opt to sacrifice an opportunity to learn something new in order to demonstrate that they are indeed smart. Far from being resilient in the face of difficulty, children who believe that intelligence is limited tend to fall apart quite easily and quickly when they encounter a challenging problem, especially if their confidence is low. Instead of trying out different ways to solve a problem, they may, for example, try the same ineffective strategy over and over again. Even if they previously experienced some success with a similar problem, they will denigrate their ability to complete the task, saying things such as "I was never good at this kind of stuff."

It should not come as a surprise, then, to find that these children tend to define intelligence in others in terms of fixed traits, saying such things as "She's smart because she always gets A's" or "He's smart because he has a big brain." (Bempechat et al., 1991). Furthermore, they tend to be overly concerned about how well they are doing in the classroom relative to their peers.

The source of these children's differing beliefs about the nature of intelligence is unclear. Children's beliefs are most assuredly influenced by their parents'—and later, their teachers'—own beliefs about children's abilities. It is also possible that, to some degree, different views about intelligence are based on children's temperament. That is to say, "easy" children may be more able and willing to subject themselves to the uncertainties that are part and parcel of new and challenging schoolwork. Both of these ideas have yet to be explored by educational researchers. We do know, however, that children's beliefs about their abilities progress in predictable ways as they grow older. John Nicholls's seminal research (1978) has demonstrated that at four to five years of age, most young children view intellectual ability as being unlimited. They agree with statements such as "The harder I try, the smarter I'll get." As early as the second grade, however, children begin to perceive ability as a fixed trait that, by its very nature, limits what they can accomplish. At this point, children begin agreeing with statements such as "The harder I have to try, the dumber I must be." Nicholls refers to this change over time as a progression from the belief in ability as "mastery through effort" to the belief in ability "as capacity," that is, limited by what children perceive as an upper limit on their intelligence.

Nicholls (1989) has argued eloquently that competitive classrooms, characteristic of the majority of public schools, serve to make children overly concerned and worried about how smart they are, which ultimately makes them focus on the products of learning— test scores and classroom grades—at the expense of understanding the processes involved in learning. In contrast, classrooms organized around cooperative learning tend to provide an environment in which children tend to be more interested in monitoring their own progress, independent of that of others. Thus cooperative learning environments focus children on how much their performance in school improves over time.

Preparing Children for their Roles as Students

Prior to beginning preschool or elementary school, children are being prepared by their parents in many subtle ways for their upcoming years in school. In most cases, parents are probably not aware of the degree to which they impart critical information about the values they place on their children's education and the behaviors that they expect from children beginning their roles as students. In some families, it is obvious that children have been prepared to meet the demands of the teacher and the school as a whole. Teachers find that there is more or less of a match between the skills and attitudes that have been taught and encouraged at home and those that will be fostered in the classroom.

In other families, however, it is equally obvious that children have been prepared differently for the beginning of school, in ways that do not necessarily match the teacher's demands for learning and expectations for behavior. Teachers find that these are often the children who have difficulty fulfilling their potential, fall behind, and develop attitudes about school that are not conducive to learning.

How do parents go about the task of preparing their children for schooling? Educational research has focused on two aspects of parent involvement that are critical for school success. The first involves *academic support* and refers very broadly to the ways in which parents foster their children's intellectual or cognitive development. Examples of this include helping children with their homework and teaching them how to prepare for tests. The second involves what I have come to call *motivational support* and refers to the ways in which parents foster the development of attitudes and approaches to learning that are essential for school success. This includes communicating the notion that learning is a process, that mistakes are a part of this process, and that persistence is key in school success. While some educational research has found that high achievement results from a combination of academic and motivational support, the research I report here shows that the former is not a necessary precursor to the latter.

WHY STUDY CATHOLIC SCHOOLS?

It is impossible to be interested in the achievement of poor and minority students without scrutinizing the success that Catholic high schools have had in educating this segment of the student population. There are many ways to measure academic achievement prior to and following high school completion, including grade point average (or GPA), SAT scores, graduation from high school, and acceptance into college. In all these ways, poor African American and Latino students in Catholic high schools outperform their peers in public and secular private high schools (Bryk et al., 1993; Coleman & Hoffer, 1987).

As I mentioned in Chapter One, it has not been easy for educational researchers to study the influence of Catholic schools on the academic achievement of minority students. The topic itself is rife with controversy, largely because of what researchers refer to as the problem of *causality*. Do Catholic schools foster higher achievement, or are high-achieving students choosing to attend Catholic schools? Indeed, the educational benefits that are associated with Catholic schools may be due to factors that have little to do with the schools themselves. Put another way, do minority students excel in Catholic schools because of better teaching, higher expectations, and consistent discipline and structure? Or are minority students who attend Catholic schools better students to begin with? It is worth repeating that it is indeed entirely possible that parents who choose Catholic over public schools may be more committed to academic excellence and thus more involved in their children's school progress than parents who do not make this choice.

Notwithstanding these concerns, it is particularly interesting that higher achievement is brought about despite what is considered to be very traditional and ordinary teaching (Bryk et al., 1993). Indeed, the innovative instructional techniques and assessments that educational researchers have been proposing as part of the large-scale efforts in school reform have not really touched Catholic schools. Further, in an educational climate that emphasizes the critical importance of embracing and celebrating ethnic and cultural diversity in the classroom, Catholic schools have, in fact, paid relatively little attention to issues such as the development of ethnic and racial identity (Delpit, 1996). Finally, it is an undisputed fact that the academic success of poor and minority students in Catholic schools is attained with significantly smaller financial resources than those expended in many other educational environments (Groome, 1998).

I believe strongly that self-selection—the notion that it is the higher-achieving students who are selecting Catholic over public education—is not as critical an issue as some have argued, nor as critical as it may have been at one time. Faced with the same decrease in enrollment as public schools, Catholic schools do not pick and choose the best students available. Increasingly, they are engaged in active recruitment of students that do not necessarily fit the stereotypic vision of motivated students from motivated families. On the contrary, Catholic schools achieve their greatest success with students who are the *most* disadvantaged (Bryk et al., 1993). Nor, as some critics have argued, are Catholic schools able to expel students on a whim, keeping only the brightest and most motivated. They are as subject to litigation as public schools, and expulsions are rare occurrences (Sister Ann Dominic Roach, personal communication, July 18, 1990).

With these considerations in mind, I was disappointed to find that very little of the research on the school performance of minority students in Catholic schools has examined children's motivation to achieve. I chose to go beyond an accounting of higher achievement, which I feel has been clearly established, to examine children's beliefs about the causes of success and failure. I was specifically interested in knowing whether Catholic school students might be more likely than their public school peers to understand success and failure in ways that are conducive to higher achievement. For example, might they be more likely to view the causes of success and failure as being within their control? And how might such beliefs be related to their actual performance in mathematics?

THE CULTURES AND
CONTEXTS OF LEARNING

High achievement in diverse ethnic groups cannot be understood in a vacuum. Influential scholars such as Vygotsky (1962, 1978), Haste (1993), and Rogoff (1990) have urged educational researchers to consider that the cultural and historical context of parents and children plays a critical, vital role in shaping and guiding the development of their beliefs about how the world works. In his discussion of cultural psychology, Shweder (1991) notes that humans constantly seek to make meaning of their contexts. Indeed, the society in which individuals live, as well as its social-historical background, continuously influences thinking and reasoning.

This means that, in multiethnic societies such as Canada and the United States, it is entirely inappropriate to force one group's way of thinking and reasoning about academic achievement on other ethnic groups. In any given ethnic group, parents may have ways of encouraging school achievement that run completely counter to the strategies of parents in other ethnic groups. As Drago-Severson suggests, for example, what Puerto Rican parents do to get their children to do well in school may have little meaning to the sensibilities of Indochinese parents (Bempechat & Drago-Severson, 1998). It is not surprising, then, that cultural psychologists are arguing increasingly against the wisdom of making assumptions that similarities or differences "across communities, across individuals within communities, or across practices carried out by the same people" can be used to describe groups or individuals other than those under study (Rogoff & Chavajay, 1995, p. 871).

I add to this that we need to move away from treating members of one ethnic group as if they all share the same beliefs about child rearing and education. Educational researchers must make greater efforts to understand how members of the *same* ethnic group differ in their child-rearing beliefs, especially those that are related their children's schooling. I have found that high and low achievers within a particular ethnic group clearly differ from one another in their beliefs about the causes of success and failure. It stands to reason that high-achieving members of a given group must also differ from one another in their understandings of the causes of success and failure in school.

WHAT DID WE DO, AND WHAT DID WE FIND?

Toward this end, my colleagues and I surveyed, across a five-year period (1990 to 1995), over one thousand fifth- and sixth-grade African American, Latino, Indochinese, and Caucasian children in poor neighborhoods in and around the Boston area, in both public and Catholic schools. Specifically, we sought to understand ethnic differences and similarities in children's beliefs about the causes of success and failure, their perceptions of their parents' child-rearing practices, especially as related to schooling, and the relationship of these to mathematics achievement. Our results call into question common assumptions about the factors that are believed to be influential in school performance.

Myth: Poor Parents Are Uninvolved

Contrary to the popular view of poor parents as uninvolved in their children's schooling, we have found that, regardless of ethnicity, all children report that parents intervene in important ways when their children's performance is low. According to the children's reports, their parents engage in effective aspects of both academic and motivational support when faced with their children's difficulties in school.

Myth: Beliefs in Effort Are Associated with Higher Achievement

Our research brings into specific relief a major misconception that has been associated with the research on the achievement of American as compared to Asian children, especially in mathematics and science. In this work, much of which has been conducted by Harold Stevenson and his colleagues, research findings have shown that Asian mothers and children, as compared to their American counterparts, believe much more strongly in the value of effort over ability in school performance. Stevenson has failed to present evidence directly linking beliefs in effort to higher achievement, yet he has effectively advanced the view that the higher achievement of Asian students is the *direct* result of their greater value on effort.

My findings show decisively that this connection does not exist. Instead, the work confirms what many other researchers of children's motivation have reported, namely that higher achievement is associated with beliefs in *ability*, not effort. Specifically, we demonstrate that, across ethnic groups, high achievers (including Asian American students) tend to believe that success in mathematics is due to their innate ability in math and not to the effort they invest in math. In contrast, low achievers, regardless of ethnicity, tend to believe that failure is the result of lack of ability and not lack of effort. This means that the relationship between beliefs about effort and ability and achievement in mathematics is far more complex than has been previously presented. I believe that we lack a more subtle understanding of this issue because researchers of achievement across cultures have neglected to consider their findings in the context of the broader research literature on children's motivation.

The Latino Paradox

We uncovered a puzzling paradox involving the perceptions and beliefs of the Indochinese and Latino students in our studies. Specifically, we found that—relative to African American and Caucasian students—Latino and Indochinese students hold very similar views of their parents' child-rearing strategies, especially as they relate to education, and reason in similar ways about the causes of success and failure. For example, both groups of children reported that their parents talk a lot about the importance of effort in learning and indicated that they feel guilty about the sacrifices their parents make for their educations. Both groups of students also believe strongly that failure in mathematics is not due to lack of ability. Yet the differences between these groups in achievement outcome are striking. The Indochinese students were the highest and the Latino students were among the lowest achievers in math. Why would beliefs that are conducive to learning be associated with high achievement in one group and low achievement in another?

The Motivational Impact of Catholic Schooling

Our comparisons of public and Catholic school students demonstrated that, relative to their public school peers, African American and Latino students in Catholic schools reason about the causes of success and failure in ways that are more conducive to learning.

For example, Latino Catholic school students are more likely than their public school peers to attribute their achievements to high ability. Of course, as I mentioned earlier, our research does not demonstrate that the Catholic schools these students attended are the *cause* of these beliefs. This leaves us with several questions. First, does high achievement foster beliefs in high ability as the cause of success, or does the belief that one has ability foster high achievement? Does the Catholic school environment foster these beliefs about high ability, or are students who elect Catholic schooling more likely to believe that they have high ability? These are not easy questions to answer. In the larger context of what we know about the achievements of minority students who attend Catholic schools, I believe that the environment of Catholic schools may very well foster positive beliefs about achievement.

With the next chapter, we begin a discussion of parents' child-rearing practices, especially as they relate to education. How do parents get their children to do well in school? What strategies do they employ, and how might this differ as a function of ethnicity? And, to what extent might high-achieving children across ethnic groups report similar child-rearing practices?

. . . .

3

The Critical Role of Parents

Few parents would deny that their children's education is a top priority. Even fewer would be pleased with poor school performance. Yet some parents meet the challenge of socializing their children for schooling with more success than others. How do parents of successful children get their youngsters to do well in school? What do they say to them, what do they do at home that fosters a genuine commitment to academic excellence? And how might this vary as a function of culture and ethnicity?

To be sure, these questions, phrased as they are, assume that children are passive recipients of their parents' entreaties, which is not at all the case. As every parent and teacher knows, children have their own individual temperaments, which exert an important influence on their attitudes about schooling. Educational researchers do not yet understand this influence on achievement very well, but we do know that among both the well and poorly educated are parents who report that they do nothing at all—that their children seemingly always demonstrated an interest in learning and have shown themselves to be highly self-motivated. At the same time, it is conceivable that parents such as these are indeed saying and doing things of which they may not be aware. As educational researchers, we struggle to make sense of what may be the relationship between parents' understandings of how they foster their children's achievement, subtle though these may be, and their children's academic performance.

TWO SIDES OF THE SAME COIN

Contrary to popular views, poor and minority parents are quite concerned about and involved in their children's school progress (Lareau, 1987, 1989). Many do the same kinds of things that have been documented in white middle-class parents, such as monitoring daily homework and maintaining close and consistent links with the teacher. What is it about practices such as these that contribute to achievement? Educational researchers are as yet unclear about exactly how involvement of this sort influences children's achievement. Researchers are also unclear about how these kinds of parental practices might differ across ethnic groups.

As I mentioned in Chapter Two, parents influence their children's academic achievement in two connected and complementary ways, by providing *academic* and *motivational* support for learning. Studies of academic support tend to ask, How do parents foster the intellectual skills that children will need to succeed in school? What strategies do they employ to teach them new skills? In contrast, research on motivational support tends to ask, How do parents encourage the kinds of motivational approaches to learning that are conducive to success in school, such as persistence in the face of difficulty? I discuss the distinctions between academic and motivational support more finely in the upcoming section and then examine the degree to which our accumulated knowledge speaks to the experiences of families across ethnic groups.

ACADEMIC SUPPORT

Much of the work on academic support has been heavily influenced by the noted and influential theories of Lev Vygotsky (1962, 1978) and Jean Piaget (1926, 1963) and assumes that parents are fundamentally teachers. From this perspective, the teaching that parents do is not necessarily spelled out in explicit ways, nor does it necessarily involve intentional techniques. Rather, the kind of teaching that parents engage in is seen as occurring in many subtle and indirect ways, and is part and parcel of the daily life and routines of families, such as tidying up after playtime or putting away groceries. For example, Sigel (1985) has studied how parents encourage the development of abstract thinking in their children, which is related to higher achievement in school. He has proposed that differences in how parents foster the ability to think in abstract ways may account for the differences that teachers often notice in children's readiness for school. In his studies of how parents teach their children, Sigel has found that some parents are more demanding than others in the ways that they encourage abstract thinking. According to Sigel, some parents make more of an effort than others to stretch their children's thinking. For example, in the course of reading a book to their children, most parents ask them to make observations about the story and point to pictures. In addition, some parents go a little further by asking their children to suggest alternative explanations for a character's behavior or to think of different strategies that might resolve a character's conflict. Observations and labeling are considered less demanding on a child's thinking than the process of proposing alternatives and offering strategies for conflict resolution. Sigel argues that parents who engage in the latter are actually facilitating the development of their children's ability to think abstractly, which ultimately makes them better prepared for the beginning of formal schooling.

In related research on school readiness, Barbara Rogoff and her colleagues have proposed that one critical aspect of the interactions between parents and their children lies in the guidance that parents provide in finding connections between new problems that their children do not know how to solve and problems with which their children have some familiarity (Rogoff & Gardner, 1984). Rogoff likens this process to a scaffold, a framework that provides physical support as an individual climbs. With such verbal scaffolding, parents facilitate the learning of new skills by controlling the level of difficulty of the task in question, providing advice, and actually showing their children different kinds of strategies for solving a problem. In doing so, they serve as models for how to cope with new and challenging tasks. In other words, parents behave much like experts. They tacitly help their novice children by creating a context in which new information eventually becomes consistent with the skills and knowledge that the children already possess.

The benefit of this kind of support is that children can use the scaffold of their parents' assistance to help them complete a task that they may not otherwise have been able to accomplish on their own. As I mentioned earlier, Rogoff stresses that parents may not (and probably do not) have explicit instructional goals but may structure these kinds of learning opportunities in subtle ways that promote their children's intellectual development. Ideally, children should work on a new skill at a comfortable but challenging level, with parents gradually adjusting the scaffold for learning, or their threshold for helping, as children acquire the new skill. Tasks that are either too easy or too difficult will not result in any new learning; the former will likely bore, and the latter will likely frustrate. In the optimal sense, parents manage their supportive behavior and interactions to levels just beyond what their children might accomplish on their own.

Not surprisingly, the kinds of academic support that Sigel and Rogoff have documented tend to be associated with social class. For example, studies of middle- and working-class mothers have shown that the former tend to ask the higher-level questions that I mentioned earlier when their children are trying to solve a problem and that middle-income children tend to have higher levels of abstract thinking than their working-class peers. However, social class by no means dictates the ways in which parents will work to foster cognitive development. Educational research is rife with examples of the ways in which middle-income mothers, anxious to ensure their children's school success, are overcontrolling in their teaching styles, ultimately heightening worries over performance and suppressing their children's intellectual curiosity. David Elkind (1988, 1994) has eloquently discussed this type of "miseducation" and its nega-tive consequences for children's motivation.

At the same time, studies that have examined differences in teaching among parents with similar backgrounds appear to suggest that, relative to mothers of low-achieving children, those of high-achieving children may be more effective tutors. For example, Scott-Jones (1987) found that among a group of low-income African American first graders, mothers of higher achievers tended to mix learning into daily household activities, supplied more books, and in anticipation of later schooling, set appropriate academic goals for their children to accomplish. In contrast, mothers of lower achievers seemed to choose for themselves a more formal, almost "teacher-like" approach to instruction, yet often made statements that indicated that they had low expectations for their children's learning.

In a related vein, others have found that families of preschool-ers who later become *successful* readers encourage their children's conversations, provide more explanations when their children ask them questions, teach them the alphabet, and play school with them. Families of children who later become *poor* readers tend to discourage conversations, especially if they are initiated by their children.

MOTIVATIONAL SUPPORT

In theory, children can arrive at school armed with all the intellec-tual skills they will need to succeed. They will not reach their potential, however, if they are prone to beliefs about and behaviors in school that are not conducive to learning, such as a lack of per-sistence, a preference for easy over challenging tasks, or a tendency to fall apart at the first sign of difficulty.

Early research in the area of parental influences tended to focus on general aspects of parent involvement. For example, some of this work showed that higher achievement is associated with the degree to which parents pressure their children to excel in school and stress the authority and status of the teacher (Haggard, 1957; Rosen & D'Andrade, 1959; Toby, 1957). More recent educational research is characterized by a finer emphasis on understanding the influence that parents' own views and beliefs have on the development of their children's views and beliefs about schooling. A growing research literature has shown that parents' own beliefs, attitudes, and values about learning serve to guide their behavior with their children around school-related issues (Eccles, 1983; Entwisle & Hayduk, 1988; Phillips, 1987). There is little question but that parents' school-related beliefs are critical for their children's academic self-esteem. They have a strong and perhaps even causal influence on their children's developing beliefs about learning. That is, the beliefs that children develop about learning may in fact result from their parents' own beliefs.

For example, Phillips (1987) showed that among a group of very high-achieving children, perceptions of academic skills were more influenced by their *parents'* beliefs about their abilities than by the children's *own* objective records of achievement. This means that among highly competent children, there are those whose academic self-esteem is more dependent on their parents' beliefs about their abilities than their own test scores or school grades.

Elsewhere, researchers such as Susan Holloway (1988) have shown that parents' beliefs about their children's mathematics ability have a profound influence on the children's self-evaluations of their own ability, their beliefs about the causes of success and failure in math, and their attitudes toward mathematics. This is apparent in the very different beliefs about success and failure that mothers hold for their sons and daughters. Mothers tend to attribute math success in their boys to innate ability, and in their girls, to effort. Where failure is concerned, mothers tend to view failure in boys as resulting from a lack of effort, and in girls, from lack of ability.

In Chapter Two, I discussed the importance of believing that performance in school, whether successful or unsuccessful, results from influences that children perceive to be internal and controllable. Seen in this light, then, it is clear that boys and girls receive very different messages from their parents about their abilities in mathematics. The message to boys is that they are smart and can control the extent to which they fail through their own efforts. In contrast, girls hear that they can try harder, but given their lack of innate ability, it may not be possible for them to stave off failure. It is not surprising that relative to boys, girls tend to believe that math is much harder and of less general use (Parsons, Adler, & Kaczala, 1982).

The Value of Encouragement

Interestingly, educational researchers have found that very obvious ways of providing academic support, such as helping children with their homework, may not be an absolutely necessary ingredient of successful children's backgrounds. Instead, several studies have shown that motivational support is a key factor in the school achievement of many poor and minority children. These findings emanate from both retrospective and ethnographic research studies—that is, from studies in which successful adults recall the influences that shaped their academic and career paths, and those in which an educational researcher observes a family or group of families in depth. Both kinds of research have documented a wide variety of support measures on the part of parents, relatives, or other adults (such as teachers), which are perceived to be enormously helpful in fostering achievement. These range from the general, such as unequivocal support for schooling and higher education, to the particular, such as helping with applications to graduate school (Harrington & Boardman, 1997; Levine & Nidiffer, 1995).

For example, in individual interviews with twenty-one high-achieving adolescents, Edwards (1976) found that students recalled that, although their parents could not provide much help with homework because of their own limited educations, they strongly encouraged their children to do well in school. Further, these students reported similar support for schooling from siblings, members of the extended family, teachers, and school counselors. In addition, their beliefs about academic success included many statements about the importance of education for their futures and a strong belief in the education ethic. For example, the students in this study strongly agreed with the statement "Blacks who work hard achieve as much as whites."

ETHNICITY AND PARENTAL SUPPORT

In light of the increasing diversity of the school-age population, educators are very interested in knowing about the role that culture plays in parents' support of their children's education. Accordingly, educational researchers have attempted to fill this gap in the research by studying how cultural backgrounds influence the kinds of academic and motivational support that I have discussed earlier and whether there are ethnic differences in the child-rearing practices that are most related to education (Ogbu, 1995; Slaughter-DeFoe, Nakagawa, Takanashi, & Johnson, 1990).

It is problematic to assume that all members of a given ethnic group would share *one* way of thinking about their children's education. Nevertheless, educational researchers and cultural psychologists have found that, as a whole, some ethnic groups, such as Indochinese and Latinos, tend to place the needs of the group—the family or community—above the needs of the individual. In these cultural contexts, adults emphasize collective goals such as family unity, respect for elders, sharing, and caring (Delgado-Gaitan, 1992; LeVine, 1977; Suarez-Orozco & Suarez-Orozco, 1995). In contrast, other ethnic groups, such as some Caucasian subgroups, tend to place the needs of the individual over the needs of the group. In this cultural context, parents tend to raise their children to be autonomous, achieving, and assertive of their individual goals and rights as family and community members (Greenfield, 1994; Holloway, Gorman, & Fuller, 1988).

This has led some researchers to argue that for ethnic groups that place a premium on family or community concerns, the goals of child rearing and the goals of schooling may actually run counter to one another (see Greenfield, 1994). That is, because education is very competitive and focused on *individual* achievement, it may unwittingly undermine the collectivist goals of the family.

However, to assume negative outcomes because of cultural discrepancies such as these is problematic. It is true that the *average* school performance of some ethnic groups exceeds that of others, but it is clear that academic excellence is not specific to any one group of children. Clearly, regardless of ethnicity, parents of successful children find ways to moderate the demands of the school, which reflects society's individualistic orientation, with their own cultural socialization goals. In my work with parents and children of different cultures and ethnic backgrounds, I chose to understand what parents do and say to their children that might help or hinder them as they work to meet the demands of the school.

Prominent researchers such as Laurence Steinberg and Sanford Dornbusch (1992) and Wendy Grolnick (1994) have made important contributions to our understanding of parental influences in children's schooling. My research differs from the work of these scholars in that I designed my studies on the foundation of theories of children's motivation to succeed in school. I was guided by a general premise that *regardless of ethnicity*, children who excel in school may have parents who provide the kind of motivational support for learning that I have been discussing—motivational support conducive to learning. As a researcher, I asked, Would high-achieving children *in all ethnic groups* report hearing the same things from their parents? Conversely, would there be some parental beliefs and behaviors specific to a *particular* ethnic group?

My colleagues began their search for the answers to these questions with students whom they knew to be high achieving—

Asian American summer school students at Harvard University (Mordkowitz & Ginsburg, 1987). Mordkowitz acknowledged that, while not a random group by any means, it was nonetheless an instructive starting point for understanding what students recall and perceive to have been important aspects of their parents' motivational support for learning. As they were growing up, what did their parents say and do to encourage academic achievement?

In general, Mordkowitz and Ginsburg (1987) found that students recalled that their parents said and did things that seemed aimed at reinforcing the value of effort and the importance of education. For example, the students recalled that their parents regulated their time by supervising their study habits, limiting their extracurricular activities, and refraining from assigning household duties so as to free up time for study. Parents frequently discussed the relationship between effort, schooling, and success in life, and also supported academic activities by providing resources such as calculators and workbooks. Interestingly, many parents did not provide specific help with homework. It is conceivable, though, that the ways in which they structured their homes and children's lives around schooling may have served to foster motivational beliefs, such as the importance of persisting in the face of difficulty, which are conducive to learning (Choi, Bempechat, & Ginsburg, 1994). These students spoke openly about the financial sacrifices that their parents had made in providing them with the tools and resources they needed to excel in school. From an emotional point of view, this knowledge seemed to go hand in hand with a deeply felt obligation to do well in school as a means to repay their parents for their sacrifices, coupled with feelings of guilt and shame over what the students themselves perceived to be substandard performance.

To what extent might the powerful recollections of these young adults have served to motivate them to excel in school? Might we tap into similar observations in younger children? Using the interviews that Mordkowitz conducted as a starting point, and taking into account contemporary theories about children's motivation, we developed the Educational Socialization Scale (ESS) to assess children's views of what their parents say and do around issues of schooling—their perceptions of their parents' academic and motivational support for schooling.

THE EDUCATIONAL SOCIALIZATION SCALE

The ESS is a questionnaire that taps into children's perceptions of their parents' academic and motivational support for learning (see Appendix). The first version (Bempechat, Mordkowitz, Wu, Morison, & Ginsburg, 1989) was developed largely from the insights we gleaned from the interviews reported in Mordkowitz and Ginsburg (1987). In developing the items, we relied heavily on the words that the college students themselves had used to describe their childhood experiences. We capitalized on the students' personal awareness of their parents' school-related attitudes and behaviors, focusing on the rather straightforward remarks they made about the extent to which parents helped with homework, discussed the relationship between school success and later life outcomes, and controlled out-of-school activities. Here are some sample items:

- My parents (or someone else at home) help me with my homework.

- My parents talk about what I can be when I grow up.

- My parents won't let me do what I want until I have finished my homework.

In assessing the frequency with which the children perceived the occurrence of their parents' efforts to provide academic and motivational support, we were mindful of the need for a scale of possible responses that was appropriate for our fifth- and sixth-grade students. We decided to structure the responses in ways that make sense to children between ten and twelve years of age, and so we asked the children to indicate the frequency with which their parents would do or say things related to education using the following responses:

Almost every day

About once a week

About once a month

About once a year

Never

The first version of the scale (ESS I) included sixteen items. In keeping with accepted practice in educational research, we conducted a first run-through of the scale, so to speak, to ensure that low-income students in different ethnic groups understood what we meant by each of the statements and possible responses. Our subsequent studies were conducted with different groups of children. A statistical grouping of the items, or factor analysis, revealed that they sorted into three primary factors: *Value*, which included items that assessed children's perceptions of the frequency with which parents discussed the value of education; *Teaching*, which examined children's perceptions of the frequency with which parents helped with homework; and *Control*, which tapped children's perceptions of the frequency with which parents controlled their after-school time.

During the course of this work, we learned more from the children about the beliefs that their parents conveyed to them, and we revised the questionnaire to take into account other kinds of parental academic and motivational support, again using the students' own words and ideas, as the following examples show.

- My parents make me feel ashamed if I do poorly in school.

- My parents say that if I don't do well in math and science, I won't get into a good college.

- I feel guilty about how hard my parents work to give us a good education.

- My parents say it's important to try hard in school.

A new analysis of how the items—now numbering seventeen—were grouped revealed five distinct clusters of statements: *Future* included children's perceptions of how often their parents commented about the relationship between education and the future; *Effort* included perceptions of how often their parents stressed the value of effort; *Guilt* included statements of guilt that the students felt over the sacrifices they perceived that their parents made for their educations; *Teaching* again included reported parental assistance with schoolwork; and *Shame* included students' perceptions of how often they perceived their parents made them feel ashamed if they did poorly in school (Bempechat & Williams, 1995; see Appendix). The children's responses did indeed document distinct ethnic differences in perceptions of parents' academic and motivational support for schooling.

CHILDREN'S PERCEPTIONS OF PARENTS' ACADEMIC SUPPORT

We have consistently found patterns of academic support that, on the surface, appear to be counterintuitive. On average, African American and Latino children report significantly *more* assistance from parents than their Caucasian peers, yet these minority students are among the lowest achievers. And Indochinese children, who are the highest achievers, report significantly *less* parental assistance relative to African American, Latino, and Caucasian children. What do these findings mean?

It is quite conceivable that lowest achievers are the ones who tend to seek out their parents for help—after all, they are the ones who need it. Children who are doing well in school are less likely to need help with homework on a daily basis. In spite of these perceptions of greater assistance with homework, the African American and Latino students performed relatively poorly on the math test. What might this mean? According to the scholar John Ogbu (1990), the answer may lie in understanding the influence of the peer group. In a study of low-income African American mothers, Ogbu found that they reported that they are very active in encouraging their children's intellectual development. They taught their children the necessary skills for school readiness, supervised their day-to-day school progress, and believed that they were having a positive influence on their children's cognitive skills. Regrettably, however, these mothers believed that their efforts seemed for naught once their children entered the third grade. Beyond that point, mothers remarked that it became increasingly difficult to counter the influence of the street. As Ogbu writes, early cognitive socialization was not an inoculation against later school failure for the children of these hard-working and well-intentioned mothers.

The fact that the Indochinese students—the highest achievers—have the lowest scores on perceptions of parental help with schoolwork could be attributed to lack of English proficiency on the part of their parents. This explanation is unsatisfactory, however, because we would expect the same to hold for Latino parents, the majority of whom were also less proficient in English. Instead, we view this finding as being consistent with two complementary notions. First, as Newman and Stevenson (1990) suggest, these students probably do not need the help, given that they are achieving at a high level. Further, they may receive academic support from their siblings and their peers, a factor that would not have been revealed by the Educational Socialization Scale as we constructed it. Indeed, several researchers have documented the ways in which Asian American children serve as academic supports for one another, for example, by getting together after school to do homework in the company of friends (Caplan, Choy, & Whitmore, 1992; Steinberg, Dornbusch & Brown, 1992). Later, this practice becomes more formalized with the formation of regular study groups in high school and college (Fullilove & Treisman, 1990).

It is very important to keep in mind that we do not know whether parental assistance, when it is reported by children, is in fact initiated by the child or by the parent. I believe that this is a promising line of research to follow. Particularly where academic achievement is concerned, it would be very interesting to show, for example, that assistance initiated by children is more effective in fostering success than assistance initiated by parents. As I will show in the following chapter, Bernard Weiner (1994), Sandra Graham (Graham & Barker, 1990), and their colleagues have found that unsolicited help from an adult can be interpreted as an indication of low ability. That is, many children are led to conclude that they must not be smart, since the adult in question felt the need to offer assistance.

CHILDREN'S PERCEPTIONS OF PARENTS' MOTIVATIONAL SUPPORT

We have found ethnic differences in children's perceptions of their parents' efforts to provide motivational support, and these differences are consistent with the children's contexts and cultures. It appears that minority parents exercise more control over their children's free time. For some groups, guilt and shame are powerfully communicated, the relation of education to the future is frequently articulated, and the importance of effort is pointedly acknowledged.

Perceptions of Parental Control

Relative to the Caucasian children in our samples, the African American, Latino, and Indochinese students perceived that their parents exercised greater control over their time outside of school.

I remind the reader that we did *not* interview parents, and so our interpretation of this finding is of course speculative. However, it is conceivable that the minority parents in our sample felt the need to exercise greater control over their children's whereabouts, given the relatively unsafe neighborhoods in which these children live, as well as the tendency of immigrant and minority parents to be concerned about negative peer influence (Kao & Tienda, 1995; Reese, Balzano, Gallimore, & Goldenberg, in press).

Perceptions of Parental Emphasis on Effort, Education, and the Future

When we compared the perceptions of Latino, Indochinese, African American, and Caucasian children, we found that the Latino students felt that their parents emphasized effort more frequently and stressed more often the role that a good education would play in their futures. It is possible that, as compared to Caucasian parents, Latino parents may be communicating a more urgent message about the importance of schooling, a notion that is consistent with parental responses to the experiences of immigration (Matute-Bianchi, 1991; Suarez-Orozco & Suarez-Orozco, 1995). We are not proposing that Caucasian parents are cavalier in their educational socialization practices. Rather, as Jimenez has noted (Bempechat, Jimenez, & Graham, 1997), given the losses associated with immigration and the encounters with prejudice that are likely to ensue, Latino parents may experience a heightened need to communicate the necessity of attending seriously to schooling.

To the extent that this is true, why did we not observe comparable differences among the Indochinese relative to the Caucasians and African Americans? Wu (1992) has proposed that the values of scholarship and hard work, so deeply embedded in Indochinese culture, provide a family context in which they may not need to be explicitly proffered—they may be already internalized. There is some support for this notion in recent studies of academic achievement among Indochinese immigrant and Chinese American,

Korean American, and Japanese American students (Caplan et al., 1992; Schneider, Heishima, Lee, & Plank, 1994). For example, Schneider and her colleagues found that there existed a mutual understanding between parents and children that the pursuit of good grades had its own intrinsic merit. Parental expectations for high grades were not verbally communicated. Rather, it was an "unquestioned expectation" that students would do their homework, attain high grades, and plan to pursue a college education.

Perceptions of Guilt and Shame

Relative to African American and Caucasian students, Latino and Indochinese students hold very similar views of the degree to which their parents foster feelings of guilt and shame in the face of poor performance. Specifically, the Indochinese and Latino children displayed stronger perceptions of guilt over parental sacrifice than the African American students. Further, Indochinese and Latino children had stronger perceptions of parental shame over poor performance than African American children had; the perceptions of the Indochinese children in this regard were also stronger than those of their Latino and Caucasian peers.

These beliefs are consistent with a collectivist orientation toward child rearing, which I discussed earlier. Both guilt and shame are prominent emotions in these two cultures. Upholding the family honor and "saving face" are primary concerns in a culture that values interdependence (see Mordkowitz & Ginsburg, 1987; Suarez-Orozco & Suarez-Orozco, 1995).

MOTIVATIONAL SUPPORT AND INTERDEPENDENCE

It has been often argued that what cultural psychologists call *familism*, or the tendency to place family togetherness over individual goals, inhibits parents' academic and motivational support for learning, especially in Latino families. Our findings do not support this view. Rather, we have shown that parental emphasis on the individual achievement of their children is not necessarily incompatible with child-rearing goals that are collectivist in nature. In this connection, Valenzuela and Dornbusch (1994) argue that the concept of familism is actually quite similar to James Coleman's notion of "social capital," in that it encourages "networks of interaction and resource exchange that facilitate the transfer of physical (material resources), cultural (cultural and linguistic backgrounds acquired to meet the demands of the school), and human (educational attainment) capital" (p. 22).

As researchers, we seem to lean toward dichotomies when we try to characterize beliefs and behaviors, perhaps because it is so very difficult to account for the complexity of individuals. As Jimenez (Bempechat, et al., 1997) suggests, however, it is more appropriate to view individualism and collectivism along a continuum and to try to understand the many and varied ways that parents adapt their cultural values so as to incorporate their child-rearing goals with the goals of the school.

4

Children's Understanding
of Success and Failure

Parents, teachers, and classrooms themselves are enormously influential in children's developing beliefs about the causes of success and failure. As I stated in the previous chapter, parents are very effective communicators of their own beliefs, so much so that many children give more weight to what their parents believe about their abilities than to the more objective indications of their skills as evident in their test scores or report card grades. In this context, it becomes important to ask how parents' efforts to provide academic and motivational support might influence children's beliefs about the causes of success and failure. In other words, are there particular means of academic and motivational support that are associated with certain beliefs about success and failure?

If parents manage to communicate their beliefs about learning to their children, it follows that teachers must also convey their personal views about what it takes to do well in school and what causes success and failure in the classroom. How do children make sense of their teachers' views about success and failure?

At a broader level, schools themselves are characterized by varying philosophies of teaching and learning. The academic success of minority students in Catholic schools raises a critical question: Given that Catholic schools have a clear philosophy about teaching that is rooted in religion, is it possible that parochial as compared to public schools communicate messages about the causes of success and failure that are conducive to learning? Is there something unique about the structure and environment of Catholic schools that has a positive influence on children's maturing beliefs about the causes of success and failure?

All these issues take place against the backdrop of a family's ethnic and cultural background and experiences. It is not possible to gain a sense of how poor and minority children understand the causes of success and failure without probing the role that culture might play in influencing parents' and children's beliefs about success and failure in school. It is conceivable that distinct cultural beliefs about learning and education foster different views of the importance of effort and innate ability in school success. In conveying these beliefs, parents send a message about what they think it takes to do well in school. The question for educators is whether ethnic groups differ in particular ways in their reasoning about success and failure in the classroom and whether this has a differential impact on their children's performance in school.

In the following sections, I will examine school and cultural influences in children's beliefs about the causes of success and failure. To summarize briefly, my colleagues and I did indeed find specific ethnic differences in children's beliefs about the causes of success and failure. However, we did not find that any one group of students was more inclined than another to embrace beliefs that are *not* conducive to learning. Instead, we found that children in all groups adhered to aspects of both positive and negative beliefs. In addition, we showed that when compared to their public school peers, minority students in Catholic schools embraced a set of beliefs about success and failure that were much more conducive to learning.

SCHOOL INFLUENCES

There are a great many aspects of schools that have an enduring influence on the development of children's beliefs about learning. A great deal of educational research has focused on how teachers foster positive or negative self-perceptions of ability. In addition, many educational researchers have focused their attentions on the structure of schooling, particularly the effects of learning in competitive versus cooperative classroom environments. And, as I have mentioned previously, the success of ethnic minority children in Catholic schools has given rise to a rather extensive literature on the academic influences of parochial schooling. I examine each of these in the following sections.

Teacher Behavior

Children cannot spend as much time as they do in our classrooms without developing an understanding of how teachers themselves understand the reasons that underlie each child's successes and failures. In studies of children's interpretations of hypothetical stories about teachers' reactions to students' success or failure in the classroom, Bernard Weiner and his colleagues have shown that children are very sensitive and attuned to the subtle messages that teachers convey in the process of giving feedback to their students (Weiner, Graham, Stern, & Lawson, 1982).

Weiner and Graham have found that children as young as five years of age can infer a teacher's belief about the cause of success or failure from his emotional reaction to a student's performance. For example, if a teacher is angry with a student because he failed a test, children assume that it must be because he did not study enough. In contrast, if a teacher feels sorry for a student because she failed a test, children infer that it must be because the student does not have the ability to learn the skills in question.

This has profound implications for how children come to understand the causes of success and failure in the classroom. In the first instance, the teacher's anger serves to communicate that the student's failure was due to a cause that was entirely within the student's control. According to Weiner, the implicit message is that this student can do much better, and the teacher's anger serves to communicate that he expects the student to do much better on the next test. By comparison, in the second instance, the teacher's pity serves to convey the belief that the student's failure is due to something over which she has no control. The implicit message in this case is that the student probably cannot do much better in subsequent tests and that the teacher does not expect much better performance in the future.

Weiner has also shown the converse to be true. Children infer the teacher's emotions from the beliefs that she conveys about the cause of a child's success or failure. In other words, when reading a story about a teacher who insists that a failing student must try harder, children will tend to assume that the teacher is angry. If the story recounts a teacher who provides positive reinforcement to a failing student for aspects of schoolwork that are not related to intellectual ability, such as neat handwriting, children will tend to infer that the teacher pities the student (Barker & Graham, 1987; Graham & Barker, 1990).

The Structure of Classroom Learning

Teachers do not communicate their beliefs about the causes of success and failure in a vacuum. On the contrary, teachers convey their views in the context of a classroom, and the way in which they choose to structure their classrooms has a critical impact on children's beliefs about the causes of success and failure. As I mentioned in Chapter Two, John Nicholls has shown how classrooms that are structured around competition create an atmosphere in which children become overly concerned with how they are doing relative to their friends, which in turn makes them very anxious about mistakes and failure. Students tend to become focused on *whether* rather than *how* they can accomplish a task. Learning becomes an exercise in attaining a desired product—the one right answer. Under these circumstances, many children come to see mistakes and failure as condemnations of their abilities.

In contrast, classrooms that are structured around cooperative learning tend to minimize children's worries about how smart they are relative to others and focus them on learning for the sake of learning and increasing their own skills and knowledge. In cooperatively based classrooms, children are more likely to focus on *how* they can accomplish a task. In this kind of classroom, mistakes and occasional pitfalls are viewed as necessary components of learning, and children tend to view learning as a process that involves sustained effort. Under these circumstances, many children come to view mistakes and failure as opportunities to learn.

Catholic Versus Public Schooling

There is most definitely something going on in Catholic schools that is compensating for the educational disadvantages that one ordinarily associates with poverty, such as low parent education, English as a second language, and single parenthood. As I mentioned in Chapter Two, Catholic schools are not generally recognized as sites of innovative teaching, nor are they noted for embracing the latest notions in educational reform. On the contrary, Catholic schools have built their reputation for academic distinction by adhering to a relatively straightforward doctrine of excellence, rooted in profound faith and a covenant to both educate and elevate the poor and disadvantaged (Groome, 1998). From the first recorded parish school in 1782 (St. Mary's in Philadelphia) through widespread growth from 1830 through 1960 and continuing to the present day, Catholic schools and their personnel have dedicated themselves to the advancement of the most disadvantaged students. This mission has not wavered in the face of the great social upheavals of postmodern society—fragmentation of the extended family, soaring divorce rates, and increasing numbers of mothers in the workplace. In fact, in its peak year, 1965, 12 percent of all American elementary and secondary school students were enrolled in Catholic schools. More recently, 51 percent of private school students in the United States are currently enrolled in Catholic schools. (I am indebted to Sister Lourdes Sheehan for sharing this information at an invited address at Boston College, April 30, 1998.)

Educational researchers who have studied the success of minority students in Catholic schools have tended to focus on high schools, largely because of the availability of great amounts of information in the form of national surveys. For example, the study known as High School and Beyond, sponsored by the U.S. Department of Education, has been conducting surveys of thousands of students every two years since 1980. This effort has provided educational researchers with a unique opportunity to study adolescents' school experiences and academic achievements in their sophomore and senior years, and beyond. Information has been collected on students from all kinds of ethnic and cultural backgrounds in all kinds of schools. This has allowed researchers who are interested in Catholic schooling to examine a variety of factors that they believe are associated with high achievement and to draw comparisons between public and parochial schools on these very factors (Bryk, et al., 1993; Coleman, Hoffer, & Kilgore, 1987; Marsh, 1991).

An accumulated body of research has now converged to show that the success of Catholic schools can be attributed to three important influences. The first is the overall teaching philosophy that pervades a Catholic school. According to Groome (1998), Catholic education is "for life for all" (p. 10). His humanistic view of education is fostered by a deeply held belief in the ability of all students to succeed. As school leaders, principals articulate a clear vision of Catholic education and provide faculty and staff with opportunities for spiritual growth (personal communication, Sister Lourdes Sheehan, April 30, 1998). Having accepted this tone for the school, teachers are focused on establishing appropriately high expectations for their students, holding each to a high standard, and providing the academic support that will enable students to meet the school's standards. As Groome (1998) states, the essence of education means "not focusing on shortcomings as if they define persons, expecting the best rather than the worst, challenging and developing gifts more than trying to correct faults, favoring forgiveness over punishment" (p. 98).

Recalling the discussion in Chapter Three about parental academic support, I believe that Catholic school teachers also operate much like experts to their novice students, serving as human scaffolding for academic enrichment in optimal ways. I like to contrast this metaphor with the occasional panicked pronouncements of public school officials about the sorry state of children's achievement. Now and again, such individuals will declare that they are raising standards yet again in an effort to raise academic achievement, as justified by the notion that students will rise to the levels educators expect of them. What many public school officials fail to grasp is that there is nothing magical about higher standards. Children will not rise to meet great expectations just because someone says so. They will, however—as they do in Catholic schools—attain enviable levels of proficiency when the academic support exists to help them meet the school's goals and standards.

In a collection of retrospective essays on their experiences in Catholic schools, several African American scholars speak of these expectations and standards as stemming from teachers' deeply held conviction that one's only salvation from prejudice and discrimination comes from academic excellence (Irvine, 1996; Shields, 1996). These scholars now recall the subtle but powerful messages they received from their teachers about the importance of hard work and sacrifice as *the* means out of poverty.

The second major influence noted by educational researchers relates to the ways in which Catholic schools are structured. In general, their organization is akin to what educational reformers refer to as *school-based management*. In other words, faculty and staff, relatively unfettered by the layers of bureaucracy that characterize public schools, solve their problems at the building level, so to speak, and hold themselves accountable to their constituents—their parents and students (Bryk et al., 1993).

The third important influence speaks directly to what is taught. Catholic schools adhere to a strictly academic core curriculum, and every parent, child, and teacher works toward the same goal—college preparation and admission. Where separation of students by ability level occurs, a practice known as *tracking*, there are few differences in the quantity and quality of subject matter that is covered (Gamoran, 1988)—students in lower tracks also follow an academically rigorous program of study.

I reiterate that I am fully aware of the difficulties inherent in drawing comparisons between public and parochial schools. However, I believe that these major influences that distinguish Catholic from public schools may indeed encourage beliefs about the causes of success and failure that are conducive to learning.

EFFORT AND ABILITY
THROUGH THE EYES OF CULTURE

Throughout this book, I have been highlighting the very profound influence that culture has on how parents and children come to understand the meaning of effort, innate ability, and the relationship between the two. In Chapter Two, I introduced John Nicholls's finding that children's understanding of the relationship between effort and ability changes with age. Recall that prior to the second grade most children believe that the harder they try, the "smarter" they will become. This linear belief often shifts to a compensatory view, as many children come to believe that the harder they have to try, the "dumber" they must be. By the beginning of the second grade, many children believe that they will have to try to make up or compensate for whatever they lack in innate ability by investing more effort in their learning—and that this effort may well be beyond them.

Imagine, if you will, how children would feel about the relationship between effort and ability if they did not believe that some people are born smarter than others. If everyone is born with more or less the same intelligence, then the only reason that could explain the higher achievement of some children would be *effort*— that internal, unstable, and controllable factor in learning about which Bernard Weiner has written so much.

Scholars such as Harold Stevenson (1993) and Susan Holloway (1988), who have studied Western and Eastern views of intelligence, have noted such distinctions in parents' and children's conceptions of ability and effort. Western culture, with its emphasis on the type of individualism of which I spoke in Chapter Two, adheres quite strongly to the view that some individuals are endowed at birth with greater abilities than others in many domains, including intelligence, and this is what ultimately explains differences in educational and career attainment. From this perspective, as Nicholls has argued, intelligence is limited by one's *capacity* and effort can only go so far in helping a student overcome lack of ability.

In contrast, Eastern culture, with its greater emphasis on interdependence, tends to view individuals as endowed relatively equally, and individual efforts and strength of character as ultimately responsible for later differences in educational and career attainment. From this perspective, as Nicholls suggests, ability is perceived as *mastery through effort*. It is not surprising, then, to learn that the concept of effort in Japan and China is closely linked to the formation of character. According to White and LeVine (1987), a major goal of child rearing in Japan is to encourage children to be "committed to and positively engaged in disciplined effort" (p. 59). The child-rearing beliefs of Japanese parents illustrate a commitment to fostering strengths of character that are essential for school success. For example, Japanese parents believe that character is molded by *ki*—the will to live; *tamashi*—the determination to overcome obstacles; and *seishin*—the mental attitude that helps a person embark on a task. Parents also believe that character is shaped by experiences of hardship, endurance, effort, and sustained struggle. These notions about character formation are the heart of motivational support for learning, which I raised in Chapter Three. I believe that Japanese parents who work to encourage such beliefs are providing their children with motivational support. They are effectively preparing their children to endure hardship, academic and otherwise.

In point of fact, many Japanese parents specify the ability to *endure hardship* as a characteristic they want their children to have as adults (Lee, 1987). This notion of enduring hardship figures prominently in the national school policy: "It is desirable that, in the lower grades, one should learn to bear hardship, and in the middle grades, to persist to the end with patience, and in the upper grades, to be steadfast and accomplish goals undaunted by obstacles or failures" (White, 1987, p. 17). This approach to character formation continues throughout children's careers in school. For example, it has been widely reported that college entrance requirements in Japan are grueling and arduous. Yet those who succeed are not said to be the "smartest"; they are said to have the strongest will and character.

As transmitters of culture, parents of course communicate these different views to their children, and there is no doubt that these views have a very different impact on how children come to understand the notions of effort and ability. In Eastern culture, the view that individuals can always improve and expand on their skills and knowledge is very powerful and tends to foster the belief that while innate ability may direct the rate at which knowledge is acquired, it does not in the least limit what individuals can achieve, provided they are diligent in their work (Chao, 1996). This is why, Holloway argues (1988), that beliefs such as these foster a sense of self-control and personal responsibility in learning. It may also explain why students maintain a long-term view of their education—many believe that years of devotion to studies will pay off (Schiller & Walberg, 1982).

I believe that this view of ability may create a more important conviction—if ability is malleable, then the only sensible thing to do is to invest effort in learning. Seen in this light, effort be can be perceived as truly enhancing one's abilities (see Bempechat, et al., 1997; Stipek & Gralinski, 1991). In other words, effort can serve to *activate* one's ability, as Lauren Resnick (1995) has suggested. It is not surprising, then, to find that Asian mothers and their children tend to home in on effort (or the lack of it) rather than ability (or the lack of it) when explaining school performance (Stevenson, Lee, & Stigler, 1986).

In contrast, the Western view of ability as *capacity* leads inevitably to what Martin Covington has called the "double-edged sword" of effort. For many children who have absorbed the Western view, admitting the necessity of exerting effort is akin to conceding lack of ability. As Covington has shown, effort now ceases to be a useful tool and becomes an implicit condemnation of one's intelligence (Covington & Omelich, 1979). It should not be surprising, then, that American children and their mothers, while extolling the virtues of effort, nonetheless tend to invoke lack of ability over lack of effort in explaining failure in mathematics (Stevenson et al., 1986).

THE CAUSES OF SUCCESS AND FAILURE: WHAT DO POOR AND MINORITY STUDENTS BELIEVE?

As researchers, my colleagues and I found ourselves treading on relatively new ground, since there are so few studies of these beliefs in poor and minority children. Educational researchers have tended to focus rather narrowly on the views and beliefs of white middle-class children and then inappropriately compare these views to those of ethnic minority poor children. This kind of research harkens back to the "deficit model" approach to educational research, about which I spoke in Chapter Two. It is of little use to teachers, largely because it erroneously assumes that the beliefs of the former are more conducive to learning than those of the latter, and as Graham (1994) has argued, it does not at all contribute knowledge that teachers could find useful in the classroom. It would be much more helpful to provide teachers with information about how high- and low-achieving children *in the same ethnic group* differ in their beliefs about the causes of success and failure. This is, in fact, what our research program attempted to do, and I discuss our findings in the upcoming sections.

Assessing Children's Attributions

My colleagues and I adopted the well-known and widely used Sydney Attribution Scale (SAS) to measure children's beliefs about the causes of success and failure. The SAS was developed originally by Herbert Marsh and his colleagues (Marsh, Cairns, Relich, Barnes, & Debus, 1984) to assess children's beliefs about the causes of success and failure in their general academic work, as well as their specific performance in reading and mathematics. We elected to use the mathematics section of the SAS, whose eleven items depict brief hypothetical stories of success or failure in the classroom and ask children to attribute the success or failure to ability, effort, or external causes, as demonstrated in Exhibit 4.1.

Our choice of the SAS was not random. It is a very reliable scale that has enjoyed widespread use among educational researchers, largely because it does not force children to choose between effort or ability or external factors in making their judgments. Questionnaires that require children to make such choices compel them to make trade-offs, depriving researchers of the opportunity to understand how children think about their academic performance in a broader sense. The SAS paints a more complete picture of how children reason about the causes of success and failure.

Ethnic Variations in Children's Attributions for Success and Failure

Over a series of studies, we did indeed document ethnic differences in how children think about the causes of success and failure. As noted earlier, however, we did not find that any one group of students was more inclined than another to adopt beliefs that would

Exhibit 4.1 Sydney Attribution Scale (SAS), Mathematics Section

The teacher needs to count the money for the class trip, and she asks you to do it. This is because:	Very true for me	True for me	Neither true nor false	False	Very false
She knows I am careful in my work.					
It was my turn.					
I am good at this.					

The teacher asks the students to swap books to correct math, and no one wants your book. This is because:	Very true for me	True for me	Neither true nor false	False	Very false
Everyone knows I make mistakes.					
I'm not good in math.					
Nobody likes me.					

Source: Marsh et al., 1984.

undermine their success in school, such as the notion that failure is due to lack of innate ability. Instead, we found that children in all the ethnic groups we studied had beliefs that were both positive and negative. In addition, we discovered that, relative to minority students in public schools, those in Catholic schools held beliefs about success and failure that were indeed more conducive to achievement.

Indochinese Students

We found that the Indochinese children tended more than their Caucasian and African American peers to blame failure on lack of effort, which in the context of the discussion of cultural factors, is consistent with their fierce commitment to effort and belief in ability as changeable (Caplan, et al., 1992). We were puzzled, however, to find that Indochinese students blamed failure on lack of ability to a greater extent than their Caucasian peers. This is even more intriguing in light of the fact that the Indochinese students, as a group, were the highest achievers on the math test. What might this mean?

My reflections on this puzzle led me back to the questionnaire—the Sydney Attribution Scale (SAS). The fact that the SAS asks students to respond to *hypothetical* scenarios may explain these seemingly contradictory findings. By definition, these hypothetical stories are far removed from the reality of children's daily lives, and the reality for these children is that they do try very hard to succeed in school. The failures depicted in the SAS were not their own—they were invented, so to speak, and the students had to respond. When presented with failure as a *fait accompli,* they may have felt that lack of ability was the only reasonable explanation. Such is the difficulty posed by questionnaires; as researchers, we have no way of knowing the varied ways in which students are likely to interpret the questions. As I will argue later on, future research of this nature may want to consider asking students to assign credit or blame to their *own* success and failure experiences.

Latino Students

Latino students had a greater tendency to credit success to effort than their Caucasian peers. And, when compared to their African American peers, Latino students believed more strongly that failure results from lack of effort. Several scholars have written that the experience of immigration tends to foster beliefs in the importance of self-reliance (Delgado-Gaitan, 1994; Suarez-Orozco & Suarez-Orozco, 1995). From this perspective, it is possible that we were witnessing the reactions of students who are socialized to understand that concentrated effort is a necessary ingredient in school success (Matute-Bianchi, 1991).

African American Students

The African American students were more likely than their Caucasian peers to blame failure on lack of effort. As I have noted, this kind of thinking has a positive influence on children's achievement because it focuses them inward on aspects of learning over which they have control. Yet these students were also more likely than their Caucasian and Latino peers to blame failure on lack of ability, a belief that is potentially debilitating because it is largely viewed as an internal and stable aspect of the self over which they have no control. However, I will argue further on that it is not necessarily a bad thing to attribute failure to lack of ability—it may indeed be perceived as a liberating experience.

Catholic Versus Public School Students

We discovered three findings in our comparisons of Catholic and public school students that support the view that Catholic schools may be encouraging their minority students to develop positive beliefs about the causes of success and failure. First, we found that, relative to their public school peers, Latino students in Catholic schools believed more strongly that success is due to ability. Second, both Latino and African American students in Catholic schools were much less likely than their public school peers to believe that success could be attributed to external factors such as luck. Third, African American students in Catholic schools were much less likely than their public school peers to believe that failure could be due to external factors such as a difficult test.

To bring some understanding to these findings, Drago-Severson (Bempechat & Drago-Severson, 1998) has suggested that Catholic and public school students may have very different perspectives on the connection between their homes and their schools (Martin, 1992; Snow, Barnes, Chandler, Goodman, & Hemphill, 1991). Specifically, she has proposed that school type—Catholic or public—may in fact have a different influence on different ethnic groups. For Latino students, the home environment appears to be as important as (or more important than) the school in supporting students' beliefs about the causes of success and failure. For African American students, the type of school they attend appears to be central in supporting their positive beliefs about success and failure.

For example, we found that Latino students in Catholic and public schools did not differ in blaming failure on external causes. In other words, they did not differ in the degree to which they accepted responsibility for failure. Drago-Severson believes that, regardless of school context, values of faith and hard work play an important role in the child-rearing practices of Latino parents. In essence, the Latino students in our studies, the majority of whom are Catholic, may have the benefit of hearing similar, positive themes about success and failure in their Catholic homes and their Catholic schools. Therefore, where positive messages about success and failure are concerned, it may not matter whether Latino students are enrolled in public or Catholic school—they are exposed to these messages all the same.

In contrast, Caucasian and African American students may not encounter the same kind of continuity in beliefs between home and school that might be experienced by Latino students. Among the African American students, those attending Catholic schools were *less* likely than their public school peers to blame failure on external factors and *more* likely to attribute success to ability—a pattern resembling that of their Latino Catholic school peers. These convictions about success and failure are positive, in the sense that they focus students inward on factors that are stable and within their control, such as effort.[1] For the African American students in our sample, then, the

---

[1]As noted, ability is widely perceived by students to be an uncontrollable factor (Weiner, 1994). At the same time, ability attributions for success are strongly associated with higher achievement, perhaps because students may need to believe they have ability in order to justify exerting effort in a given academic domain (Stipek & Gralinski, 1991).

Catholic school environment may indeed encourage them to assume more personal responsibility for their intellectual development. This notion is consistent with the overall teaching philosophy of Catholic schools, discussed earlier, which stresses individual accountability and personal responsibility. This notion is also supported by personal reports of Catholic school teachers, who have stated that they feel a special obligation to push their children to reach beyond their intellectual potential through hard work and resistance to negative peer pressures, including those that might undermine school achievement and individual effort (Polite, 1996; York, 1996).

Again, I reiterate these findings do not speak to the issue of causality. It could very well be that Catholic schools foster adaptive beliefs about schooling and learning. Alternatively, since Catholic schools are essentially schools of choice rather than schools children are required to attend, newly enrolled students may already have positive beliefs about the causes of success and failure. Again, however, decreasing school-age populations have affected all schools, and Catholic schools have had to market their own benefits in an effort to fulfill enrollment goals. It seems more reasonable that a combination of school and family factors contribute to fostering beliefs about success and failure that are conducive to learning.

CHILD-REARING PRACTICES AND BELIEFS ABOUT THE CAUSES OF SUCCESS AND FAILURE

How might parents' child-rearing practices be related to children's beliefs about the causes of success and failure? My studies found that moderate to strong associations between parental practices and children's beliefs that are consistent with theories of children's motivation to achieve. First, my colleagues and I found that children who perceived that their parents stressed the relationship between education and the future tended to believe that success results from personal effort. Sounding a cautionary note, however, it could be that parents who focus their children on the connection between present school performance and future life outcomes may foster beliefs about the importance of effort.

Second, we found that parents who were perceived by their children to stress the value of effort in learning tended to have children who strongly believed that failure was due to lack of effort *as well as* lack of ability. That is, children who perceived that their parents stressed the importance of sustained effort tended to attribute failure to both lack of ability and lack of effort. While motivation theory would predict that the former could be debilitating, it may not necessarily be so, especially in combination with the latter.

Third, parents who frequently helped their children with homework had children who believed that success was due to external factors and not innate ability. They also tended to believe that failure was due *both* to lack of ability and lack of effort. As we discussed earlier, children who perceive that they are the subject of frequent assistance tend naturally to believe that they need the help; after all, if they had the ability, they would not need the assistance. In this context, it stands to reason that they make the link to this combination of beliefs about success and failure (Barker & Graham, 1987; Graham & Barker, 1990).

Fourth, children who perceived that their parents were more often ashamed by poor school performance tended also to blame failure on lack of ability and lack of effort. In contrast, children who perceived less shame from parents over poor performance tended to credit success to ability and effort.

It is very tempting to draw causal links from these findings. However, it is simply not clear whether children's perceptions of their parents' academic and motivational support for learning fosters the beliefs about effort and ability that we documented, or whether children's beliefs about success and failure engender parental behavior of the kind that these children perceived. This a clearly an area in need of careful research, and I will propose possible avenues for educational studies in Chapter Eight.

5

. . . .

Success in Mathematics

Our heightened awareness of the lamentable state of children's achievement in mathematics is due largely to the efforts of two noted scholars, Harold Stevenson and Robert Hess. Since the mid-1980s, their teams of cross-cultural researchers have been documenting the exemplary mathematics achievement of elementary and high school students in Asia, most notably those in Japan, Taiwan, and the People's Republic of China. Their findings have highlighted deficits in learning that are not limited to one area of mathematics: Unfortunately for all of us—parents, teachers, and educational researchers alike—the lags cut across all subject areas, including fractions, algebra, geometry, measurement, and probability (Stevenson, Chen, & Lee, 1993; Hess, 1991).

The recent Third International Mathematics and Science Study (Beaton et al., 1996) added more grist to the mill of underachievement in its comparison of math competence in students from forty industrialized nations. This extensive study showed that the overall mathematics performance of American eighth graders, for example, is significantly inferior to that of their peers in half of the forty nations sampled, including France, Austria, Japan, and Singapore. In contrast, American students outperformed their peers in seven participating nations, including South Africa, Columbia, and Romania, countries where civil unrest and social upheaval have arguably affected children's education for the worse.

In the United States, there is no question that educators have witnessed improvements over the past several years in math achievement among ethnic minority students. Despite these gains, however, African American and Latino students continue to display lower *average* standardized test scores relative to their Caucasian and Asian American peers (Mullis & Jenkins, 1988). For example, the National Educational Goals Report (1995) included tests of the degree to which fourth-, eighth-, and twelfth-grade students were able to perform at "proficient" or "advanced" levels based on standards defined by the periodic testing of the National Assessment of Educational Progress (NAEP). The report showed that in the eighth grade, for example, the percentage of African American and Latino students who met the Goals Panel's performance standard in mathematics was well below the percentage of Caucasian and Asian/Pacific Islander students who did so. Among these students, 3 percent of African American, 8 percent of Latino, 44 percent of Asian/Pacific Islander, and 32 percent of Caucasian students met the performance standards. Thus, while improvements have occurred, much work lies ahead for students and educators.

And yet mathematics is far from the only subject that our children study in school. Why are we witness to such anxiety about mathematics? Clearly, the answer lies in the fast-paced technological changes that have occurred over the past two decades. The economies of industrialized nations rely increasingly on a workforce that is proficient in technologically relevant skills, whose foundation lies in mathematics. No nation can afford to risk its competitive strength with students who are ill prepared to meet the challenges of our increasingly global economy.

UNDERSTANDING UNDERACHIEVEMENT

Awareness of the distressing state of mathematics achievement among elementary and high school students has led educational researchers to sharpen their examination of math competence in poor and minority children. This kind of scrutiny is long overdue. In recent years, teachers and educational researchers have perceived an increasing need to understand the underrepresentation of girls in higher-level math courses in high school, which results in a narrower pipeline of female math majors in college and the eventual underrepresentation of women in careers involving math and science. While these concerns are undoubtedly justified, the emphasis on gender differences in mathematics has taken needed attention away from the state of math achievement among ethnic minority children. These are the very children who risk being excluded from the workplace that awaits them. Thus, we have an urgent need to understand the factors that foster or hinder children's advancement in mathematics.

Educational researchers who have confronted this problem have noted several influential factors that account for the glaring disparities in cross-cultural achievement in mathematics. Cultural attitudes toward learning, which I raised in Chapter Four, are critical in the different levels of achievement that researchers have documented. While it is somewhat dangerous to generalize to entire peoples, there is nonetheless something to be said about the ways in which learning and learnedness are valued in Eastern as compared to Western cultures. This is reflected in the degree to which teachers and the teaching profession as a whole are held in very high esteem and are rewarded in Japan, for example (White, 1987).

From my perspective, the most interesting differences are those that scholars have noted in factors that are inexorably linked to children's motivation (Chen & Stevenson, 1990; Hess, Chang, & McDevitt, 1987). Harold Stevenson and his colleagues have found that Asian mothers and their children are far more oriented toward effort than ability in explaining the reasons for success and failure than American mothers and children. For example, while Asian and American mothers both stress that effort is more important than innate ability in determining children's performance in mathematics, American mothers place much more emphasis on innate ability than their Asian counterparts. In other words, Asian mothers do not invoke ability or lack of ability nearly as much as American mothers in explaining their children's achievement.

As we discussed in the previous chapter, this greater focus on effort probably leads Asian children to the overall belief that achievement in mathematics is something that is *unstable* but *internal* and *controllable*, as Weiner has proposed. This can arguably foster resilience in the face of difficult or challenging assignments. In contrast, the greater willingness of American mothers to invoke ability or lack of ability in explaining their children's successes and failures likely encourages the view that achievement in mathematics is inevitably limited by intelligence, a trait that is *internal, stable,* and something over which students have *no control* (Weiner, 1994). It is not a far stretch to see that this orientation toward learning can foster a sense of helplessness in the face of difficulty or failure.

Second, the quality of both teaching and textbooks brings an enormous influence to bear on student achievement. James Stigler (Stigler & Perry, 1990; Stevenson & Stigler, 1992; U.S. Department of Education, 1998) has found that U.S. teaching of mathematics is organized around what educators call the "spiraling curriculum." This is the notion that with each new academic year, concepts previously learned should be reviewed before moving ahead to the current year's learning goals. Thus there is a tremendous amount of repetition, which is unnecessarily boring for many students—and somewhat comforting for others, who quickly realize that whatever they have not mastered by the end of one year will be taught again the following year.

In contrast, Japanese teachers know at the onset of a school year that whatever concepts they teach must be mastered, for there will be no opportunity for lengthy review. Thus teachers and students remain focused on advancing understanding of the year's learning goals in preparation for the next level of mathematics the following year, and textbooks reflect this orientation toward teaching and learning.

In light of these research endeavors, it is perhaps *not* coincidental that research on mathematics education picked up in the mid-eighties. The emphasis seems now to have shifted its focus onto what mathematics educators call "deep conceptual understanding"—leading to study of what that means and how it can be fostered (Cobb, Yackel, & Wood, 1992; Lampert, 1990). Schwartz (1995) distinguishes between what he calls problem *solving*, which fosters critical thinking skills, and problem *posing*, which encourages the development of exploration and conjectures. Schwartz argues that the latter has been virtually neglected in mathematics education, with the result that students may not be developing the skills they need to hypothesize and speculate.

In fact, students who can accurately and quickly solve routine problems without being able to apply their knowledge to new and different problems may be successful in conventional academic terms, but they lack a deep-seated understanding of math concepts. Increasingly, math teachers are very interested in how students take that extra step in their learning, going from "routine" learners to "adaptive" learners who have a rich conceptual knowledge of mathematics and are flexible in their application of mathematical principles (Hatano, 1988).

Many educators believe that this kind of understanding comes from teaching that fosters a more constructive view of mathematics as a domain of study. Much to the dismay of mathematicians and math educators, many children and adults see math as a subject that is driven by the memorization of facts and rules, in which there is no room for creative thinking. This is likely the result of the ways that mathematics has typically been taught and assessed. The emphasis on finding the one right answer is a perfect example of what Nicholls refers to as a "performance" orientation toward learning, a point touched on in Chapter Four. Tests and other assessments that focus on students' abilities to perform routine or rote tasks direct them away from opportunities to demonstrate the degree to which they can be flexible in their understanding of mathematics (National Mathematics Education Board, 1993).

In recent years, educators have sought to teach math in ways that foster the view that mathematics is a body of knowledge that one *constructs*, through manipulation and experimentation. While educators do indeed want successful students, they prefer not to see students succeed because they have very rigid attitudes about math and do math in very uncreative ways (Cobb et al., 1991; Lampert, 1990). In fact, some educational researchers have found that so-called unsuccessful students, traditionally defined as those who tend to do poorly on typical math tests, find very creative ways of solving math problems when unfettered by rigid rules. And students who have been successful in the traditional sense tend to falter when given the freedom to pose and explore multiple solutions to the same problem (J. Schwartz, personal communication, March 20, 1995).

This perceived need to foster a more creative and constructivist view of mathematics has developed hand in hand with the desire among many math educators to find more authentic or real-world ways to assess student achievement. Ruthven (1994) argues that, ideally, assessments should be intrinsically interesting—and can be made so if they are designed with some connection to the world in which children live. In addition, new ways of assessing math knowledge and competence should allow students to use mathematics imaginatively, encourage them to develop and interpret their own conclusions, and make it possible for them to use multiple ways to solve the problem.

The focus, then, seems to be increasingly on the *process* of learning (examining, analyzing, exploring alternative routes to varied solutions), rather than the *products* of learning (that is, the one right answer, the grade). This focus on process is exactly what leaders in mathematics education would like to see. Indeed, process seems to be the thread running through each of the five broad goals proposed by the National Council of Teachers of Mathematics (Giordano, 1993). If we wish students to value mathematics, reason mathematically, communicate mathematics, solve problems "that vary in context, in length, in difficulty, and in method," and develop confidence, then the move toward performance assessments is likely to foster the attainment of these goals.

These developments in teaching goals and assessment strategies speak to the very heart of cooperative learning, a classroom orientation that educational researchers have been advocating for some time. I believe that the move toward more authentic means of teaching and assessing mathematics will fulfill the goals of cooperative learning. For example, the focus on encouraging students to think of multiple ways in which a given problem can be solved will move them away from concerns about the so-called one right answer. This approach will also lessen the need to know what and how others are doing, since it is implicit that many possible ways of determining solutions are possible. Furthermore, in this context, mistakes are indeed necessary and valuable learning tools.

This commitment to authentic means of both teaching and assessment among mathematics educators has been the impetus behind many of the innovative mathematics education initiatives taking place around the nation. For example, the Connected Mathematics Project: Teaching, Learning, and Assessment, the Interactive Mathematics Program (IMP), MATH Connection, and Making Mathematics Accessible to All (MMAA) are four nationwide curriculum and assessment programs that have some history and that are well regarded in the mathematics education community for their innovativeness and creativity. These programs get at the heart of valid assessment by capturing student growth in understanding rather than knowledge at a single point in time. It is hoped that they will eventually become a substitute for current assessment methods, which carry with them very high stakes, such as admission to college.

These programs, all funded federally or corporately, have teacher training and support as a major component. In addition, they focus on collaborative work and foster the development of higher-order thinking skills and deep conceptual knowledge through such tools as graphing calculators, computers, and other concrete materials. Assessment methods are multidimensional, including both written and oral projects. Preliminary results are promising. For example, a five-year evaluation of the IMP initiative has found that, relative to non-IMP students, IMP students post higher grade point averages, enroll in more semesters of mathematics, and attain comparable SAT scores.

Preliminary evaluation of MATH Connection has found that the program has allowed female students to feel more empowered in their math work, has improved performance and attitudes toward math among both males and females, has closed the achievement gap between males and females, and has encouraged critical thinking through the use of journals.

These early findings bode well for the development of positive beliefs about achievement in the domain of mathematics. It is quite possible that participation in such programs might foster the motivational tendencies that are essential for school learning, in math as well as in other domains. These include persistence, diligence, and resilience to learned helplessness. I can think of no better example of this possibility than that of Uri Treisman's work with mathematics students at Berkeley (Fullilove & Treisman, 1990). In his capacity as professor of mathematics, he noticed that African American students, relative to their Asian American peers, were failing introductory math at alarming rates and that few were choosing to major in mathematics. To understand the nature of this problem, he spent time with African American and Asian American students, going to their dorms, the cafeterias where they ate, and the places where they studied. He found that students from both groups brought with them from high school the study skills that had gotten them into Berkeley. For the Asian American students, that meant forming study groups. Indeed, Treisman found that, within one week of arriving on campus, the Asian American students had formed study groups for each course in which they were enrolled.

For the African American students, in contrast, what had brought them success in high school was solitary study, away from any and all distractions (Suskind, 1998). This skill, so valuable in high school, was hurting them in college. Treisman used this knowledge to institute mandatory study groups for all students in his mathematics classes. As a result, his African American students are now thriving in math, are choosing to major in math at significantly higher rates than those that existed prior to this intervention, and have higher college persistence and graduation rates than those that existed prior to this program.

RESULTS

The best measure of the work I report in this book lies in its ability to say something useful to teachers and parents, something that can help them guide their children toward improved or sustained learning. It is not enough to document differences in parental support for learning, as I have defined it, nor is it sufficient to show how children differ in their reasoning about the causes of success and failure in mathematics. We need to be able to adequately address the question that everyone asks of educational researchers: What is the impact on actual achievement?

The questions my colleagues and I raised dealt first with the direct relationship between parents' academic and motivational support and children's math achievement. In what ways is children's performance in mathematics influenced by their perceptions of what their parents say and do around issues of schooling—their academic and motivational support strategies? It would be naïve to assume that there is one best strategy for ensuring school success. Clearly, what one child perceives as genuine parental concern can easily be the same behavior that another child perceives as relentless nagging. Add to this the influence of culture and type of school—Catholic and public—and the reader can appreciate the complexities inherent in understanding the role that parents play in fostering academic achievement. With this in mind, we focused our efforts on understanding the extent to which the relationship between parental support and math achievement might be different for different ethnic groups. In other words, might support strategies that relate to success in one group be related to failure in another group?

We then planned a second set of questions focused on children's beliefs and their math performance. Specifically, how are children's beliefs about the causes of success and failure related to their actual achievement in mathematics? And is the relationship between children's beliefs about success and failure different for different ethnic groups? That is, might beliefs associated with success in one group be associated with failure in another?

Our third set of questions focused on the comparison of Catholic and public school students. We were especially interested in knowing how the beliefs and performance of minority students in Catholic schools might differ from those of their public school peers.

In all our efforts to understand our findings, we sought to uncover not only differences between the ethnic groups, but also differences within each ethnic group. In other words, we wanted to gain a better understanding of how all these influences might have a different effect on high and low achievers within each group. I describe our findings in the upcoming sections, integrating them with the work of other prominent educational researchers.

Ethnic Differences in Mathematics Achievement

When my colleagues and I compared the math achievement of the students in each of the ethnic groups, we confirmed what many studies have shown over the years. Specifically, we found that, as a group, the Indochinese students had much higher math scores than all other students. Also, Caucasian students, on the whole, had higher math scores than their African American and Latino peers. Further, African American and Latino students had the lowest scores of the four groups, with African American students doing somewhat better than their Latino peers. While we did not find Catholic school students as a whole to be higher-achieving than their public school peers, we did discover that Latino students in Catholic schools did much better on the math test than Latino students in public schools. This means that for the Latino students in our studies, there was most definitely an academic advantage for those receiving a parochial education.

Mathematics Achievement and Academic and Motivational Support

For each ethnic group in our studies, we consistently found that children who perceived that they were often on the receiving end of parental efforts to provide academic and motivational support tended to be among the lower achievers. On the face of it, this seems odd. After all, parents who are involved in their children's schooling should see them doing well in school. Instead, we seem to have tapped into quite the opposite pattern. Regardless of ethnicity, students who did poorly on the math test reported heightened parental involvement relative to those who had scored higher. In particular, students who perceived that their parents provided relatively frequent assistance with schoolwork, often emphasized the value of effort in academic achievement, and repeatedly stressed the vital connection between education and the future tended to have lower scores in mathematics.

While this finding may seem counterintuitive at first, it actually fits in well with what educational researchers have noted about parents of low achievers. It seems that the tendency of parents may be to take an active role in their children's schooling when they show signs of poor performance. After all, as we have stated before, high achievers are not the ones who need assistance on a regular basis. Other researchers have noted this relationship between low achievement and parent involvement. For example, in a study of elementary school students in Taiwan, Lin (in Ho, 1994) similarly found that parental help with homework was negatively associated with academic performance. He argued that this reflected low-achieving students' need for parental assistance (see Newman & Stevenson, 1990). Indeed, children who are doing well in school do not need their parents' assistance. Furthermore, they may have already internalized the inherent connection between academic achievement and future outcomes, along with the necessity of investing effort in schoolwork. Our findings suggest that parents in all ethnic groups may take a reactive rather than proactive stance with regard to their children's school performance. That is, parents in general may be most likely to step in as a reaction to low grades rather than as an inoculation against future failure.

Mathematics Achievement and Beliefs About the Causes of Success and Failure

My studies have consistently found that high achievers tend to credit their performance to *ability*. In other words, they believe that success in mathematics is due to their own innate abilities, and they do *not* believe that failure could be due to low ability. This finding holds for each ethnic group. Simply put, higher achievers, no matter their ethnic background, believe that they are smart. In contrast, lower achievers in all ethnic groups tend blame failure on lack of ability and tend to credit such success as they experience to external factors such as luck.

These findings carry two important implications. First, positive beliefs about achievement are not unique to any one group of students. Nor, for that matter, are negative beliefs about achievement the province of one particular ethnic group. This finding holds despite the wide range of achievement that we documented among the students in our studies. This means, for example, that the higher-achieving Indochinese students—who as a group scored significantly higher than the African American and Latino students— adhered to the same positive beliefs about the causes of success as the higher-achieving students of the other minority groups. This also means that the lower-achieving students in all the ethnic groups, despite the great differences in their math scores, believed in the same negative views about achievement.

Second, these findings *do not* imply that high-achieving children are unconcerned about effort, nor do they suggest that these students believe that they do not need to try hard in order to succeed. As I mentioned in Chapter One, I am bound by the limits of the questionnaires I chose for these studies. Therefore, it is *only* in the context of children's responses to the Sydney Attribution Scale that their beliefs about the importance of effort were unrelated to their performance on the math test. I am certain that, had we also interviewed the children, we would have learned more about their beliefs about the role of effort and ability in their math performance. I will take up the issue of methods and their limitations in Chapter Eight.

We also discovered that Latino students who endorsed stronger beliefs in their math ability tended to have higher math scores. For these students, it may be especially beneficial to their success in school to believe that they have ability. Why is this? The answer may lie in what we know about the relationship between teacher expectations and pupil performance, a possibility that we will take up in the next chapter (Rosenthal & Jacobson, 1968; Rosenthal, 1995).

What of the beliefs of high and low achievers *within* each ethnic group? As I mentioned earlier, there was significant variation in average math scores among the ethnic groups. Yet within each group, high and low achievers differed in their beliefs about the causes of success and failure in ways that are consistent with current theories of children's motivation. For example, relative to their lower-achieving peers, higher-achieving African American and Caucasian children had a greater tendency to credit success to innate ability. And when compared to their higher-achieving peers, lower-achieving African American and Caucasian students had a greater tendency to attribute failure to lack of ability. Additionally, lower-achieving Indochinese students were more likely than their higher-achieving peers to blame failure on lack of ability.

These results are consistent with Weiner's findings on children's beliefs about the causes of success and failure. He has suggested that the tendency to blame failure on lack of ability is potentially incapacitating, largely because, as we have stated earlier, innate ability tends to be perceived by older children and adults as a trait that is internal, stable, and over which one has virtually no control. When children view the causes of failure in this light, it makes perfect sense for them to believe that effort will do little good in the long run. After all, if one doesn't have the necessary ability to succeed in a given subject area, what is the use of trying? This kind of reasoning poses a serious challenge to teachers and parents. How can we help children past this point? We will address this problem in Chapter Seven.

Our findings on children's beliefs about the causes of success and failure, resulting from our studies of ethnically diverse groups of children, largely confirm what the noted scholar Herbert Marsh (1984) has uncovered about the relationship between children's beliefs and their performance in school. He too has documented the profound influence that beliefs about ability have in predicting academic achievement. His research has not revealed a positive relationship between beliefs about effort and achievement. In fact, for the Caucasian students in our studies, higher scores were associated with a tendency *not* to attribute success to effort. This finding does contribute to the overall sense from our data that students' beliefs in their math abilities play an important role in their performance.

Further, our results are consistent with Covington's notion of effort as a double-edged sword (Covington & Omelich, 1979), which I discussed earlier. That is, while parents and teachers may genuinely believe that high effort is a virtue, they have also managed to communicate that it implies low ability. It should not be surprising, then, that high achievers come to view success as resulting from high ability.

WHAT CAN WE SAFELY CONCLUDE?

These findings show clearly that active academic and motivational support for learning is associated with lower math scores. And students' beliefs in the strength of their abilities are associated in a positive way with their performance in mathematics. I must return, however, to a critical cautionary note. Our findings say nothing about the *causes* of the students' math performance. We cannot say whether children's poor school performance leads parents to provide more intense academic and motivational support, or whether the tendency of some parents to provide a lot of support leads to lower achievement. The first of these possibilities makes intuitive sense. Parents who see their children struggling and receiving less than stellar report cards, or who acknowledge teachers' worries about their children's performance in school, are likely to do what most parents do—step in to provide assistance, either personally or with the enlisted aid of an older sibling or tutor.

The second alternative may at first seem an unusual possibility. After all, how can well-intentioned parents who provide a lot of support for learning do any harm? Unfortunately, they can indeed do more harm than good. When parents provide children with unsolicited help, they are actually communicating that they do not believe that the children can successfully complete the particular assignment on their own (Graham & Barker, 1990). In situations such as these, children are likely to begin questioning their abilities. If parents suddenly sit down to provide pointers, it must be because they think their children will "get it wrong." In many cases, however, parents' perceptions probably do not reflect reality. Overcontrolling and over-involved parents may act out of their *own* need to protect their children from mistakes and failure. They end up conveying a whole host of beliefs about learning that are potentially debilitating to future achievement, including a conviction that the most important concern in learning is to do better than everyone else in the classroom. This can only serve to generate feelings of academic insecurity in children. Indeed, parents who provide too much support or scaffolding, as we discussed earlier, are actually depriving their children of the opportunity to learn from mistakes, to assimilate these mistakes into their continued attempts to understand the given concept, and to discern for themselves the kinds of deep conceptual understandings that are the necessary building blocks for advanced learning.

With regard to children's beliefs about the causes of success and failure, we cannot say with any certainty whether doing well in school leads children to believe that they are smart, or whether students achieve more if they believe they have high ability. This argument can cut both ways. That is, it could very well be that an academic history of good grades and positive reinforcement from teachers and parents can lead some children to believe that they possess high ability. On the other hand, it is equally possible that some children simply know that they are smart, perhaps because their parents have told them so and they believe them. In this case, the power of this belief can propel them to academic excellence.

In either case, it would be very interesting to know how these beliefs may be influenced by family members. Are parents of high achievers providing the kinds of academic and motivational support that foster strong self-perceptions of ability, and if so, how? I will examine the possibilities for future research on this topic in Chapter Six.

And what can be said about the influence of Catholic schools? Undoubtedly, it could very well be that Catholic schools foster beliefs about schooling and learning that are conducive to academic excellence. Alternatively, as I have stated elsewhere, because of self-selection, children in Catholic schools may arrive with such beliefs already in place, perhaps in some cases fostered by parents' academic and motivational support strategies. My view is that, for a variety of reasons that I will take up in the next chapter, self-selection is no longer as critical a concern as it may once have been.

6

Overall Success in School

How do children at risk for school failure beat the odds? The research discussed here has highlighted critical aspects of parent involvement, beliefs about the causes of success and failure, and the kinds of schools that illuminate factors that encourage academic success. It has also raised serious questions about accepted theories of academic achievement. I will discuss each in this chapter.

RECAPPING OUR FINDINGS: WHAT DID WE LEARN?

Chiefly, our findings lend support to the small but growing literature that has shown that poor and minority parents are indeed involved in their children's schooling. From the highest- to the lowest-achieving ethnic minority groups, all the children that we surveyed perceived that their parents expressed and acted on concerns for their education, either by providing *academic* support in assistance with homework, or by providing *motivational* support through articulating beliefs in the important relationship between education and future economic survival.

According to their children, parents expressed these beliefs differently in accordance with their *specific* cultural values and the contexts in which they lived. However, where children's actual achievement is concerned, we found instead a pattern of reported parental behavior that appears to be culturally *universal*. In other words, in all the groups we surveyed, the tendency to provide assistance with homework and to stress the relationship between success in school and future prosperity was perceived as more intense by those children whose math achievement was relatively low.

In addition, the findings refute previous research that has characterized poor and minority children as being prone to beliefs about causes of success and failure that can undermine success. My colleagues and I have shown that in all the groups of children we studied, students think about success and failure in ways that can be sometimes helpful and sometimes hurtful. In our *ethnic* comparisons, no one group of children exhibited beliefs that could be construed as healthier than the others. Nor can one conclude, based on the information collected, that each ethnic group is characterized by a certain pattern of beliefs about the causes of success and failure. That is, it is not the case that one ethnic group reasons one way about success and failure while another ethnic group reasons in a completely different way.

Quite to the contrary, across all the groups, students who were higher achievers tended to credit success with their innate ability and tended *not* to blame failure on lack of ability. This finding held when we compared the groups to one another and when we compared high and low achievers to each other *in each group*. We simply cannot conclude that high achievers in a given ethnic group think in a completely different way about success and failure than high achievers in another ethnic group.

Finally, the results of our investigations suggest that ethnic minority students are at a distinct advantage when they are enrolled in Catholic schools. As I stated at the beginning of this book, it would be foolish to ignore the possibility that the Catholic school children in our studies were the most intelligent and highly motivated of the bunch. As the reader well knows, I believe very strongly that this is far from the case. I do know that in the Catholic schools we studied, students were not selected for entrance on the basis of examinations, nor were they routinely expelled or dismissed if they arrived with or came to experience academic or social difficulties. In this sense, these schools and their teachers "cope with the hand they are dealt." I believe that the extent to which this hand is an exemplary one to begin with will always be open to debate, as well it should be. I will argue for research that focuses specifically on the issues of self-selection that are inherent in any study that involves school choice, whether or not this choice is parochial.

As researchers and educators, we were puzzled by paradoxical findings in each of the ethnic minority groups we studied. The reported commitment of African American parents to their children's education is inconsistent with their children's actual performance in school, which was relatively low. So too is the shame and guilt over poor performance and parental sacrifice felt by the Latino students, who affirmed very positive beliefs about their abilities, yet were the lowest achievers in our studies. Finally, we did not know what to make of the fact that the Indochinese students—the highest achievers—believed very strongly that failure is due to lack of ability. This runs counter to so much evidence in many other studies of Asian American students. In the following section, I will present our interpretations of these paradoxes, leaning very heavily on culture and context for possible explanations.

The African American Paradox

According to their children, the African American parents in our studies were actively involved in and concerned about their children's performance in school. Despite their efforts, their children were, by our objective accounts, doing rather poorly in math. Why is this? I believe that the answer lies partly in the influence of these children's peers, an area in which we did not focus our research. As I mentioned in Chapter Three, African American mothers interviewed by John Ogbu spoke powerfully of their efforts to prepare their children for school and to keep them on track once they had entered kindergarten. By third grade, however, these mothers found themselves competing unsuccessfully with their children's peers, who became increasingly influential in distracting their children from the good study habits they had instilled in them.

This scenario appears to play itself out as children get older. Several compelling reports have emerged recently showing that high-achieving African American students pay dearly for their commitment to academic excellence. For example, Ron Suskind's (1998) account of Cedric Jenning's journey from a underfunded, unsafe high school in Washington, D.C. to Brown University is fraught with experiences of daily taunting and humiliation from peers who ostracized him for his academic pursuits. This phenomenon, which Fordham and Ogbu (1986) have referred to as "the burden of acting white," is very debilitating, leading some students to deliberately sabotage their own learning by neglecting to complete assignments and study for tests. Others find ways to hide or mask their accomplishments so as to minimize the perception that they are smart. Still others, like Cedric, increasingly isolate themselves from their peer group.

Why do successful African American students report little peer support for academic pursuits? According to Ogbu, the answer lies in these students' cultural understanding of education and achievement in society. While African American students may voice their concerns about the importance of a good education, Ogbu argues that the real-life experiences of those around them lead them to believe that formal schooling will *not* pay off in the long run. Older friends and family members who recount their frustrations with racial discrimination and job ceilings justifiably do little to foster faith in the "American Dream." In Ogbu's (1995) recent comparative study of voluntary (Chinese) and involuntary (African American and Latino) minorities, he found that African American students were very distrustful of the school as an institution and its personnel. In interviews all students reported believing in the value of education and hard work as a means of getting ahead, and the majority had aspirations for high grades. However, more than the other groups, African American students believed in "alternative sources of knowledge" (such as street knowledge and common sense) and "alternative avenues to success" (such as sports and entertainment).

Additionally, scholars have suggested that in response to a society and a system of schooling that has been perceived as inherently racist, many minority students have come to see school success as incompatible with ethnic identity (Fordham & Ogbu, 1986; Steinberg, et al., 1992). In support of this sentiment, Ogbu (1995) showed that involuntary minority youth (African American and Latino) reported much more stigmatizing of high-achieving students than did voluntary minority students (Chinese). In other words, some involuntary minority youth may experience an inordinate amount of conflict between school achievement and ethnic identity, a problem with serious consequences for children's adaptation to school (Anson, 1987; Bernal, Saenz, & Knight, 1995; Carey, 1990; Suskind, 1998).

The Latino Paradox

When the Latino students in our samples spoke of their parents' attempts to foster achievement in the classroom, they reported beliefs and practices that are consistent with a collectivist orientation towards child rearing. For example, relative to the African American and Caucasian students, the Latino students noted that their parents placed a greater emphasis on the importance of effort in academic achievement and that they felt guilty about the sacrifices their parents were making for their education. They also felt very ashamed when they did poorly in school. Furthermore, they were positive about the causes of success and failure. That is, they viewed success as resulting from high ability and, importantly, did *not* believe that failure could be due to lack of ability. In fact, these beliefs were quite similar to those endorsed by the Indochinese students. Yet, the differences between these groups in achievement outcome were striking to us. Why would these beliefs about achievement be associated with higher achievement in one group and much lower achievement in another?

The cultural and ecological contexts in which these students strive to achieve offer several possible explanations for the apparent paradox between the achievement beliefs and outcomes of these two groups in our samples. It is possible that, as DeVos (1978) has suggested, Indochinese families, as typical refugees, may be more resilient to the "adult status degradation" that is experienced by minority group members (Jimenez, 1998). As such, they may be more able than Latino families (who are more similar to caste-like minorities) to ease the "permeability of educational experiences," that is, to accept and trust in the school and its agents. From this perspective, socialization for academic achievement and socialization for collectivist goals do not appear to be incompatible. Indeed, as Greenfield (1994) has argued, the former can be pressed into service of the latter; to do well in school is to uphold the family honor.

However, different cultures understand the purposes of education differently, and this cannot be ignored, as Reese and her colleagues (in press) have shown. Their recent ethnographic study of thirty-two Latino families revealed that parents articulated the concept of education, or *educaciòn*, as a blending of both moral and educational behavior. Accordingly, these parents saw their primary responsibility as raising a moral child, teaching respect for elders, and guiding children down the right path in life. However much they valued education, these parents made it clear that they would sacrifice educational opportunities if it meant that their children might come into contact with others who could possibly be a negative influence on their social and moral development (Reese, Balzano, Gallimore, & Goldenberg, in press). They noted the particular case of a gifted adolescent girl whose parents, fearing peer influences that could undermine their parenting, refused to give her permission to attend an advanced mathematics class at another school.

The Indochinese Paradox

We were surprised to find that, contrary to previous research on Asian American students, the Indochinese students in our studies attributed failure to lack of ability much more than their Caucasian peers did. This finding is made more interesting in light of the fact that the Indochinese students were the highest-achieving group. This result runs contrary to almost every study of Asian American students that has been conducted over the past fifteen years. Many of the existing research studies have touted the fact that Asian and Asian American students are focused almost exclusively on *effort*. Researchers have documented the extent to which these students invoke the power of effort to explain success, while condemning lack of effort for failure. Why then did we find our students attributing failure to lack of ability?

As I mentioned in Chapter Four, I believe that the answer lies in the methods we chose to study these questions. Recall that the Sydney Attribution Scale asks students to respond to *hypothetical* scenarios of success and failure. Arguably, as indicated by their performance on the math test, as well as by anecdotal information provided by teachers, the Indochinese students in our studies were not failing. Yet, the Sydney Attribution Scale forces them to reason about why they *would* fail. Pushed up against this kind of wall, they may have felt that lack of ability was the only reasonable explanation. Of course, this is only speculation, but it speaks directly to the limitations of the work I present in this book. Clearly, hypothetical scenarios are far removed from the daily successes and failures that children experience. If we want a truer understanding of how children reason about success and failure, we need to talk with them about their own experiences. This may seem quite obvious to the reader, but as a matter of contemporary research, it is something that is rarely done.

THE BENEFITS OF CATHOLIC SCHOOLING FOR ETHNIC MINORITY CHILDREN

What is it about Catholic schools that might foster the positive beliefs and attitudes about learning that we documented among the African American and Latino students in our investigation? Leaving aside for one moment the issue of self-selection, to which I will return later, I believe that the overall pedagogical philosophy of Catholic schools is one that leads children to believe in their intellectual abilities and strive for academic excellence. As other scholars have noted, Catholic schools and their teachers are very much "mission" oriented (Bryk, et al. 1993). Serving and advancing the poor and marginalized in society has long been a major commitment of the Catholic church. In its schools, this calling is translated into clearly communicated structure and classroom discipline, demanding curricula, and consistently high expectations and standards for both social behavior and academic performance. The schools and their personnel are singularly focused on college preparation (Hill, Pierce, & Guthrie, 1990).

Unfortunately, it does not appear that minority students in public schools are subjected to similarly high expectations and standards for behavior and achievement. Rather, the evidence from many studies at the high school level have documented the excessive degree to which African American and Latino students are placed in lower tracks, where rote learning, busy work, and the ubiquitous "life skills" classes dominate learning. In such environments, the teaching of higher order intellectual skills, such as the ability to integrate and synthesize material from many sources, is not a pedagogical priority (Oakes, 1985). Notably, this is *not* the case in Catholic high schools, where track placement is unrelated to race and ethnicity and where the educational experience of even the lower tracked students is much more demanding when compared to public high schools (Keith & Page, 1985; Lee & Bryk, 1988; Marsh, 1991).

Of course, we did not study high school students and so cannot assume that what holds for adolescents would also hold for mid- to late-grade school-aged children. Despite this, I do not believe it unreasonable to assume that the same teaching philosophy that permeates Catholic high schools would also characterize their elementary school counterparts. This raises the question: How and in what ways do children benefit when they are held to high standards of performance? From a motivational perspective, demanding teachers and curricula communicate to children that their teachers believe they *have* the ability to learn, even if it may take some students longer than others to master certain aspects of a given subject matter.

I believe that this kind of implicit faith in children's ability to learn serves to encourage children to have faith in their *own* abilities. Over time, children may come to believe, as did the students in our investigation, that academic success is due to ability and that failure, when it occurs, is *not* the result of lack of ability. Indeed, it could be that, in their deliberate attentions to students' academic, spiritual, and personal growth (Bryk et al., 1993), teachers in Catholic high schools may provide the kinds of feedback that encourage positive attitudes about learning. For example, some researchers have shown that feedback, when used as an opportunity to also provide motivational messages ("It's obvious to me that this was last minute work—you can do much better than this"), encourages children to be optimistic about their school performance in the future (Dweck, Davidson, Nelson, & Enna, 1978). I believe that a careful study of Catholic school teachers' pedagogy would likely find this kind of motivational support, much more so than in public schools.

Given our previous discussion of peer *dis*couragement of academic achievement, it is entirely possible that students who maintain a strong conviction in their academic potential are better able to minimize disparaging comments and messages that communicate low ability. Educational researchers do not know exactly how this might happen. There is no doubt that ethnic identity is inexorably linked to students' perceptions of academic achievement, but here too our understanding is limited. Given what I have witnessed in the Catholic schools that took part in this investigation, I believe that, as organizations of faith and learning, they and their personnel work very hard to foster these convictions. However, it would be naïve to ignore other influences, such as supportive parenting, mentoring, or individual resiliency on the part of students. All of these possibilities need careful research.

In this connection, we would be remiss if we did not address a critical issue pertaining to the learning beliefs and attitudes of the Catholic school *Caucasian* students. Why is it that they did not have more positive beliefs relative to their peers in public schools? Given the extra care with which Catholic school personnel encourage the achievement of their minority students, Drago-Severson (Bempechat & Drago-Severson, 1998) has suggested that Caucasian students may not be exposed to messages about academic achievement with the same intensity as their minority peers. Given their position as ethnic majority students, it is likely that minority students receive more frequent and urgent messages about both their *potential* to achieve and the *necessity* of achieving in a racist society.

REASONING ABOUT SUCCESS AND FAILURE: QUESTIONING ACCEPTED THEORY

It is of some concern to me that the children in our studies reasoned about success and failure in ways that were completely inconsistent with findings that have been reported by the noted scholar, Harold Stevenson. Where our work found that higher achievers tend to credit their *abilities*, Stevenson and his colleagues have reported for many years that higher achievers credit personal *effort*. It is important to reconcile these differences, largely because these contradictory findings point teachers in completely different directions in their attempts to foster children's motivation to succeed.

I believe that these contrary positions reflect a desire among those who have studied the achievement of Asian students to develop a story that makes intuitive sense. And indeed, the work of Harold Stevenson and his colleagues promotes a very compelling narrative of high achievement. The story reads something like this: Chinese and Japanese cultural traditions place enormous emphasis on individual responsibility and the malleability of intelligence. In contrast, Western society is guided by a very strong cultural belief in innate ability—some children are born smart and some are not. From this perspective, it makes perfect sense that the exemplary performance of Asian children is due to culturally based, unwavering beliefs in the power of effort; by comparison, Western underachievement is naturally due to a greater willingness on the part of parents and children to invoke the critical importance of innate ability—if one lacks intelligence, there is little that can be done in the face of repeated failure. Hence, as Stevenson has argued, Asian students adhere to an "effort" model and American students to an "ability" model of learning (Stevenson & Stigler, 1992).

Regrettably, there is no available data to support this story. The research that has been conducted up until now has neglected to document the extent to which children's beliefs in effort are associated with their math test outcomes. In effect, the story of Asian excellence in mathematics is embedded in a house of cards. We simply do not have the information we need to know how Asian students' beliefs about success and failure are related to their math achievement, if at all (Bempechat & Drago-Severson, 1998).

Further compounding the difficulties with this cross-national research is the fact that the most recent international study of mathematics achievement, the Third International Mathematics and Science Study (TIMSS), found that Japanese, Korean, and Singaporean seventh and eighth graders believe much more strongly than their American peers that ability is a necessary component for success. The American students, in contrast, were no less oriented towards the value of effort (Beaton, et al. 1996). Cutting to the core of Stevenson's assertions, this investigation, which represented students in the tens of thousands, found that Asian as compared to American students are much more convinced of the necessity of *good luck* for success in mathematics.

It is ironic indeed that cross-national researchers have neglected to consider how culture influences students' understandings of success and failure. How is a question about the relative importance of effort and ability in school achievement interpreted by Japanese, Chinese, and American students? To the extent that different meanings are attached to effort and ability in these cultures, we cannot know with any degree of certainty that the same item on a questionnaire is interpreted in the same way by students from different cultures. This is a critical problem that is not limited to cross-cultural comparative research. In fact, the failure to consider the many ways in which students understand their school experiences and beliefs has seriously undercut the potential of educational research to be of real help to teachers.

In the case of any individual child, it is difficult to know what kinds of beliefs about success and failure are the most likely to foster academic achievement. If anything, the contemporary approach to achievement motivation, with its focus on how children *interpret* beliefs, makes clear that, at some level, very little is clear. The seminal work of Bernard Weiner and John Nicholls, when examined together, gives us all reason to tread cautiously when we try to understand the academic consequences attached to children's conceptions of success and failure. *Our* interpretations of *children's* interpretations depend on the degree to which we are able to understand the *context* in which these children are learning and growing. Educational researchers, myself included, have made this task that much more difficult because they have relied so heavily on questionnaires and surveys. Indeed, when we look closely at two current and influential theories of children's motivation, we can see the extent to which changes in classroom structure can lead children to reason very differently about the causes of success and failure.

Bernard Weiner (1994), whose studies of beliefs about success and failure I first discussed in Chapter Four, defines ability as a characteristic that is internal, unstable, and uncontrollable. In other words, according to Weiner, ability is a fixed trait. From this perspective, it would appear that children are best off when they attribute success to ability and failure to lack of effort. While ability is uncontrollable, it is stable and internal. It is therefore a good thing for children to believe that they are smart and that poor performance or failure is due to lack of effort, since this is a characteristic of individuals that is internal, unstable, and controllable—something that can be relatively easily rectified.

What happens if, for one reason or another, some children begin to doubt their abilities? This could be potentially debilitating; from Weiner's perspective, it would seem that children are in the *worst* possible position when they believe their failures are due to lack of ability and their successes to high effort. Both are very dangerous positions for children's academic self-concept. The inherent stability of intelligence leaves children with nowhere to go—they simply cannot get smarter. The very idea of redoubling one's efforts can only make things worse, for this becomes an implicit condemnation of their ability. They are caught by what Covington has called the "double-edged sword." That is, they know they need to try harder in order to succeed, but the very act of having to do so implies that they lack ability. However, what if by altering the structure of the classroom, one could change the way children reason about the causes of success and failure?

John Nicholls (1989) has argued eloquently that noncompetitive, cooperatively oriented classrooms can foster the view that ability is indeed changeable through effort. In cooperative classrooms, whatever concerns children have about their intelligence tend to dissipate, leaving them room to focus on the *process* rather than the *product* of learning. In these classrooms, children tend to view effort as *activating* ability; thus, it may be a good thing for children to attribute success to ability *and* effort, since the former is perceived as malleable and the latter is viewed as a helpful tool that can be pressed into the service of ability (see also Livengood, 1992; Howard, 1995; Resnick, 1995).

Similarly, it may not necessarily be debilitating for some children to believe that they lack innate ability and that effort can compensate for this innate deficiency. It is possible that believing and accepting that one is not smart is a liberating experience, especially if one also believes in the power of sustained effort. In that sense, it is much more important to be the kind of student who, acknowledging lack of ability relative to others, can initiate, maintain, and reengage oneself in effortful learning.

The Danger of False Dichotomies

I believe very strongly that experimental and questionnaire studies of children's motivation to succeed in school have exhausted their usefulness. In no way do I mean to minimize the contributions made by this kind of educational research, of which I have been a part. Rather, I am arguing that the reliance on these research methods has lead educational researchers to characterize children and their understandings of academic achievement as dichotomies—to classify them into neat packages, if you will. Researchers (myself included) have introduced us to children who are "entity" or "incremental" theorists; "performance" or "learning" oriented; "task-involved" or "ego-involved"; and "effort" or "ability" oriented. I personally have never met an "entity" boy or a "task-involved" girl. These distinctions are theoretical, and our teachers do not teach theoretical children—they teach real children. It is incumbent on educational researchers to provide them with information that they can *really* use in their classrooms.

As an example, imagine a high-achieving girl who, through her responses to Dweck's questionnaire, is classified as an incremental theorist. It makes no practical sense that this girl would be motivated exclusively by a desire to increase her skills and knowledge, no matter the cost. I cannot believe that such a child is unconcerned about how well she does on classroom assignments and tests or that she would be unfazed by a grade of C if she felt that she had at least learned something. Similarly, excepting a pathological case, who is the child who would keep himself from learning so that he could maximize high grades? Granted, Dweck has never argued that children are one or the other "kind" of theorist. In fact, she has maintained that we all have aspects of both kinds of theories within our belief structures. Yet, this is just the phenomenon that has never been studied. The tendency towards experimental studies precludes the investigation of children's achievement beliefs *in context*. In other words, if we truly want to know how children think and reason and feel about schooling and learning, we need to sit down and talk with them. This may seem absurdly obvious to the reader, but regrettably, few researchers who study children's achievement motivation take the time to talk with children.

As researchers, we have at our disposal methods that most of us have long ignored, methods that are qualitative in nature and that can provide just the kinds of theoretical and practical insights that can deepen our understandings of children's motivation to succeed in school. Research of this nature is difficult to conduct and messy at times. But such are the daily contexts in which children learn and in which their beliefs about achievement evolve. We cannot hope to understand what this means to children without trying to understand how they make meaning of their experiences in school. I will take this discussion further in Chapter Eight.

7

Lessons for Parents and Teachers

Amajor goal throughout this investigation has been to extract lessons from the findings—principles, if you will, that teachers and parents can apply to help their children reach and even surpass their current intellectual potential.

My findings and observations over the course of this investigation lead me to the following recommendations for parents and teachers. While I believe strongly in what I have come to conclude, I have an obligation to state what many of us who study families have come to know—there are multiple pathways to the same developmental outcome. As resolutely as I may adhere to certain beliefs and practices, I know they will not guarantee school success for children in all families. Nor, for that matter, will they guarantee success for all children in the *same* family. What worked for my parents and for me surely would not have worked for many of my friends. What worked for me did not necessarily work for my brother, and vice versa. The paths to success are indeed many and varied.

SET EDUCATION AS
THE FAMILY'S TOP PRIORITY

Parents talk a good game but communicate very mixed messages about the value of education. Few would claim that education is not a priority in their homes, yet for many, their actions belie their beliefs. A case in point—the *Boston Globe* recently ran a story about how parents manage their children's sports schedules. One mother spoke of the elaborate system of priorities that she had put in place for her three children, each of whom participated in more than one sport, sometimes in more than one league. In the event of scheduling conflicts, a particular sport was assigned priority over others, so that a game or practice involving the primary sport would take precedence over a game or practice involving another sport—and for a given sport, a game involving one league would take precedence over another league's practice. Needless to say, juggling all these priorities for each of her three children and seeing to it that each was where he or she was supposed to be involved organization of the highest order, with parents picking up and dropping off at all hours during the school week. For example, it was not uncommon for one child to have a 7:30 P.M. hockey game on a school night at a location forty-five minutes from her home. This would mean leaving home at 6:30 in order to allow leeway for traffic, leaving the rink at 8:30, and arriving home at approximately 9:15 P.M. At no point did this mother volunteer how dinner and homework figured into this elaborate hierarchy of priorities. I have no doubt, however, that this mother would be quite upset if school failure began to invade her home. What would she do? Regrettably, this same dilemma has been recounted to me by teachers in Boston's most and least privileged neighborhoods. The sport may differ, but the problem remains.

Some parents (the minority, I fear) would face the obvious—their children are devoting too much time to sports at the expense of academics and should be pulled off of their teams until their grades are acceptable again. One of my colleagues faced just this problem, and for her the solution was just as obvious, but in no way involved pulling her son from his hockey team. The school's guidance counselors agreed—to forbid her son from playing his favorite sport would be a horror of Draconian proportions. There was no question that her son's self-esteem would plummet, and then all of them—mother, son, school teachers, and counselors—would be facing a much more dangerous problem. All manner of problem behaviors were predicted as quite probable consequences.

I have no doubt that the teachers and counselors, speaking from many combined years of experience, have witnessed just the scenario they predicted for this teenager. After all, their views on this issue have evolved in a context in which they have seen other students and parents experience the same dilemma. What concerns me, however, is the implicit belief that this student's self-esteem can derive only from hockey, a sport in which I grant he had enviable talent. Why can't high self-esteem derive from the feelings of competence and efficacy that come from doing well in school?

Let me propose an alternative resolution. What if all parties—mother, teachers, school counselors, and student—rededicated time and effort into this student's schooling, and what if this resulted in more responsible behavior and higher achievement? Granted, this would not likely occur within one month and perhaps not even within two or three months. Maybe it would take the rest of the year and even the rest of the following year. I believe that by this time, many critical lessons about life would be learned, albeit grudgingly. First, that one needs to have a longer-term view of the future. While it is wonderful to develop athletic skills, this can only take a student so far. Second, that there are times when we all need to sacrifice something we truly love for a larger and more important goal. Surely, no one would want this boy to abandon his love of the game forever. The message is that a short-term loss will lead to a long-term gain. Third, that achievement in schooling, like achievement in athletics, comes with diligence and practice. Just as one cannot cut corners in the development of athletic ability, one cannot cut corners in the pursuit of academic skills. This kind of approach to problems in school serves the purpose of fostering the kinds of beliefs and behaviors that we all know enhance children's motivation in school, and ultimately their performance as well. I am referring to precisely those qualities that teachers work so hard to encourage and yearn to see in all students—diligence, persistence in the face of challenge, and the ability to delay gratification.

And yet I fear that some educators unwittingly undermine their own attempts to foster the development of these qualities, as the following incidents demonstrate. One of my friends recently told me that her twelve-year-old daughter revealed that she was not doing as well as she had hoped in social science. After discussing her progress, her mother told her that she would not allow her to play spring softball if her term grade was any lower than a B. Needless to say, her daughter was not happy and recounted her mother's concerns to her social studies teacher. His response? He told her that even though her term grade was to be a C−, he would give her a B because he believed that it was very important to participate in sports. Leaving aside the issue of integrity (or the lack of it), this teacher managed, with this one promise, to undermine both the girl's academic progress and her mother's parenting goals.

When the twelve-year-old son of another friend dropped from an A to a B+ in math, his mother cut back his baseball practices to once a week, so as to allow extra time for study. Imagine her astonishment when the math teacher called home to tell her that she was being too hard on her son and that B+ in her opinion is an excellent grade. Of course, these are only anecdotes, but they speak volumes about the extent of our commitment to academic excellence.

I believe that these anecdotes reflect our society's ambivalence toward academic excellence and its notions of the ideal child, or our collective "ego-ideal," as Kagan has written (1989). We want desperately for our children to be well rounded. Our ideal child is one who does well in school, participates in sports, is sociable and has many friends, and perhaps also plays a musical instrument. Is this really possible? Probably not. On the other hand, do we want children who attend to nothing but their schoolwork? Of course not. However, in my experience, without a healthy balance and clear priorities, something falls to the bottom of this list, and that something is often the rudiments of day-to-day schooling. Education cannot be one priority among several—it must be the top priority.

LET CHILDREN SUFFER

As I have discussed earlier in this volume, cultures differ in their understanding and interpretations of concepts such as effort and ability. Cultural interpretations of effort and ability guide parents differently in their child-rearing practices and reflect ego ideals that vary considerably across culture and ethnicity. In so doing, they communicate very different beliefs about the value and importance of education. The examination in Chapter Four of Japanese beliefs about how children should be prepared for schooling showed clearly the degree to which parents are concerned with their children's future ability to weather challenge and endure difficulties. There seems to be an implicit, unquestioned understanding among both parents and teachers that the ability to be resilient in the face of failure or setbacks does not develop mysteriously. Rather, these qualities are believed to evolve and strengthen over time and after much experience coping with difficult situations.

For Japanese parents and teachers, the characteristics associated with effort—the will to live, the determination to overcome obstacles, and the mental attitude that helps a person tackle a task—cannot truly develop in a context that is devoid of the experience of hardship. This conception of effort, guided as it is by culture, carries with it the understanding that one must endure hardship as a matter of course and that it is beneficial to each child's development into a responsible, contributing member of society. The hardship associated with arduous study while sacrificing pleasure is said to be good for children (White & LeVine, 1987).

Within Asian societies, effort has many meanings and is oriented toward social obligation, as Susan Holloway (1988) has shown. For example, for Chinese parents and teachers, the concept of effort implies a deeply rooted sense of obligation to one's family, one's community, and oneself. There is no doubt that American parents stress the importance of effort for improving one's school performance but not necessarily for improving one's *self*. There is simply not the same emphasis on effort as a necessary means to improve one's character. Thus, for Chinese parents and children, effort and hard work are enlisted to satisfy many varied obligations. Chinese parents, families, and communities take primary responsibility for teaching and disciplining children, and the child's achievement thus reflects the commitment of the community; it is in this sense that achievement motivation is socially oriented (Holloway, 1988).

In general, middle-class parents do not tend to speak of self-improvement in ways that encourage a sense of responsibility for society. We do not tend to see the motivation to achieve as necessarily socially oriented. In mainstream middle-class culture, a child's achievement does not necessarily reflect the achievement of the family or the community. On the contrary, the typical Western orientation toward independence is fostered in such a way that individual improvement takes precedence over societal improvement (see White, 1987).

Notwithstanding David Elkind's legitimate concerns about the "hurried child" (1988, 1994), I do not believe that the experience of suffering and the ability to endure hardship are integral aspects of many Western parents' or teachers' child-rearing concerns. Indeed, I believe that too many parents and teachers are overly preoccupied with children's happiness—to the ultimate detriment of their future capacity to tolerate challenge and uncertainty, not only in school, but in other aspects of life as well.

In my interactions with many parents and teachers, I find that they are more occupied with shielding their children from hardship, particularly where educational challenge is concerned. There is no question that this approach to teaching and learning does more harm than good. At some point in their schooling, children will inevitably encounter failure, despite repeated efforts to learn and understand. This will happen at different transition points for different children. For some, it may occur in fourth grade, when the goal of reading changes. Rather than reading for *content*, children at this point must increasingly read for *understanding*, a task many find problematic (Chall, Conrad, & Harris-Sharples, 1991). For other students, serious academic difficulties may emerge in the transition from elementary and middle school to high school, when, as Eccles (1983) has written, the environment of the school changes dramatically. No longer are children relatively sheltered in a small school, with one teacher who knows each child well. They now have to find their way in a huge building and try to forge relationships with six or more teachers, many of whom may not get to know them as individuals. Yet other students may face this point when they begin their college careers, away from the psychological safety of parents, family, and friends. As parents and teachers, we do no one—not least of all our children—any favors by shielding them from hardship.

Do we want our children to suffer for the sake of suffering? Of course not. But it is truly acceptable if our children become angry with us now and again and if they perceive us as mean-spirited for denying permission to go to the movies on a Wednesday night. They will get over it. When we make clear that school takes precedence over everything else, we are teaching our children to develop beliefs and behaviors that will be increasingly necessary as they encounter a school culture that only intensifies its demands on them as they grow. This kind of stance toward schooling conveys to children that they cannot do whatever they want, whenever they want to do it; they must learn to delay gratification. It communicates that we appreciate and expect that some subjects will be, at one time or another, very difficult to master. It also communicates that we fully acknowledge that school is sometimes boring but that this in no way excuses children from having to do what they have to do. This is the way we, as parents and teachers, expect it to be. Are we uncaring, mean, and spiteful? Absolutely not. When we approach our children's schooling in these ways, we are giving them invaluable gifts—the ability to delay gratification, to be persistent in the face of obstacles, and to maintain interest even as they dislike the work that they are doing.

My students, who are both teachers and parents, become infuriated with me when I express these opinions. After all, they say, children are only children—let them enjoy their childhoods. There is plenty of time to learn the "hard lessons of life." There is indeed plenty of time to learn life's more unpleasant realities. The real question is, will our children be prepared to cope with these realities when the time comes? The invaluable gifts of which I speak are gifts of motivation; they cannot be easily wrapped and presented like a birthday present at one time in a child's life. Like any ability, they must be nurtured over a very long period and in qualitatively different ways as children grow. We can engage in quarrels of Talmudic proportion over just *when* we should begin this process; my feeling has always been that these lessons should begin when schooling becomes more formal—in the first grade, when children begin to understand what school is all about and what is expected of them. I see no reason to save these lessons and essentially shelter our children until some later point in their growth, when serious problems with school motivation may present themselves. In this connection, it is very interesting that the successful adults interviewed by Harrington and Boardman (1997) tended to view their failures in a positive light. The authors suggest that their early and difficult experiences may have strengthened them and made them more resilient against later obstacles.

ORIENT CHILDREN TOWARD THE PROCESS OF LEARNING

Eminent researchers such as John Nicholls have argued eloquently for the need to establish classrooms that are structured around cooperative learning goals. I have both observed and participated in these scholarly debates and perceive that the trend toward cooperative learning is a slow one. The overwhelming tendency is to maintain a competitive structure. Most of the time, children are pitted against one another in a race to show who can learn material the best and fastest way. They vie for a limited number of rewards in the way of top grades and teacher recognition, and so, by definition, the majority of children are excluded from what becomes an elite club.

Given this reality, we need to find ways to communicate to children that there is more than one way to reach a solution, that it is virtually impossible to learn without making mistakes and taking the time to understand errors, and that despite all evidence to the contrary, day-to-day schooling is not a race to see who can be the first to find the right answer. When we try to accomplish this, we ask a lot of our children. We need them to embrace goals that educational researchers have unwittingly portrayed as incompatible. We do not want children to sacrifice opportunities to acquire new knowledge—but at the same time, we do want them to be concerned about their performance. We very much want children to welcome academic challenge, but we do not want them to become overly intimidated by mistakes. We want our children to try hard to excel, but we need for them to accept that there is no shame in failure. We most certainly want our children to learn for learning's sake, but they also need to know that they will have to master subjects they may never enjoy and may never need to use in their future careers.

Parents and teachers can convey these messages through example. Very few of us can attest to daily work-related activities that are *always* intrinsically interesting. Conceivably, we get through the more mundane aspects of our jobs and occasional periods of boredom because of our interest in the long-term goals we hope to attain or benefits we hope to reap. Our strategies in the service of these goals can be of critical instructional value for our children. School does not always have to—nor should it always—be fun. Learning is a process that takes time, is not always interesting, and in which mistakes are both inevitable and invaluable.

MAINTAIN HIGH EXPECTATIONS
AND STANDARDS

No one gains when teachers and schools expect different levels of academic achievement from their students. When we are differentially demanding of our children, we do everyone a disservice—our children, our schools, our communities, and certainly our society, whose childhood population is unarguably ill prepared for the technological challenges of the twenty-first century. Children are not ignorant vessels. As early as the beginning of the second grade, they know who is the smartest and who is the "dumbest" in different subjects. They are very aware of what kinds of assignments the teacher asks of different children. They know the degree to which easy work or busy work is demeaning. They are fully aware of the occasions when teachers are asking less of them than they are of others and at a very young age are able to discern that they are not getting the challenging assignments because the teacher probably thinks they are dumb. This realization is worse than benign neglect—it is motivationally incapacitating.

Barring serious learning difficulties or mental retardation, all children are able to learn and should be held to high expectations and standards for academic achievement. As I mentioned in Chapter Four, the demand for higher-quality work cannot be made without proper consideration for the contexts of the schools that children attend. A mandate for higher standards of performance is no guarantee of anything, except perhaps anger and resentment on the part of children, their teachers, and their parents. New and more stringent requirements for high school completion, for example, can be met if the appropriate supports are put into place to guide children toward the fulfillment of these standards.

Despite what parents and children may say about the delightful feeling that comes from achieving success easily, we know that both place a high value on success that emerges from struggle (see Stipek & Gralinski, 1991). And success that comes from struggle involves mistakes and setbacks, which we must help children see as a necessary part of learning.

ENCOURAGE HEALTHY
SELF-PERCEPTION OF ABILITY

If anything, the work reported here has revealed that it is healthy for children to believe that they have some measure of innate ability. This belief may very well inspire them to invest effort in their learning when they encounter obstacles. At the same time, there is no need for children who perceive that they have not been blessed with natural ability to succumb to negative attitudes about learning and pessimistic views about what they may be able to accomplish in the future.

Parents and teachers need to convey to children that effort, even of Herculean proportions if needed, can compensate for any perceived lack of ability. If some children believe that this will reveal how dumb they really are, then so be it. In some ways, it is almost a relief to acknowledge that one doesn't have the same natural gift as another in a given subject. There is a way in which this realization can free a child up to invest the necessary effort to succeed. The key for parents and teachers lies in convincing children that effort does eventually pay off. Granted, some may never acquire the deep conceptual knowledge needed to oversee the nation's nuclear power plants, or manage a Fortune 500 company, or argue before the Supreme Court. But if college entry requires Elementary Physics or Introduction to Accounting or Qualitative Reasoning, I see no reason why any student, with enough personal effort and academic support, cannot meet such requirements with distinction.

STRENGTHEN
HOME–SCHOOL PARTNERSHIPS

Teachers know that when they reach out to parents to involve them in their children's schooling, many respond very favorably. Educational researchers such as Joyce Epstein (1987) have shown that when suc-cessful models of partnership between home and school are put in place, math and reading achievement tend to increase; truancy, sus-pension, and expulsion tend to decrease; and students tend to par-ticipate more in extracurricular activities (National Educational Goals Report, 1995). There is no question that all parents need to feel that they are welcomed by the school and its teachers and counselors (Comer, 1980). This only serves to strengthen the bond between teachers and parents, who are more likely to see themselves as working partners with teachers toward a common goal of student achievement. James Comer has argued this point even further, sug-gesting that links between homes and schools must take children's families and communities into consideration. Teachers, counselors, and principals need to know their children not only as students but as members of a family—however it is defined—which in turn be-longs to a larger community. Understanding the *contexts* in which children live gives teachers and other school personnel deeper insights into each child's adjustment to schooling. This gives teach-ers freedom at many levels. For example, knowledge and under-standing of the communities in which children live gives teachers opportunities to link their curricula with community events. Knowl-edge of children's difficult home situations gives teachers the chance to offer not pity but much needed emotional and academic support that can help children, during difficult family times, maintain their learning at an acceptable level. Overall, a shared understanding of children's home and community contexts fosters a sense of school community.

LEARN FROM CATHOLIC SCHOOLS

There are many pockets of school reform in which successful part-nerships between home and school can be found. Notwithstanding these efforts, I find it very interesting that we have in our midst a model of home–school partnership that is very successful and that receives relatively little attention. Catholic schools have always embraced the view that learning cannot take place devoid of family and community concerns. The care and attention that Catholic school teachers and principals give to their constituents has resulted in enviable levels of success among the poorest and educationally most disadvantaged students. In this connection, Groome (1998) has suggested that the success of Catholic schools may have less to do with actual religion and more to do with the shared vision of the goals of schooling and the rich social capital that comes from a supportive community.

Catholic schools welcome, encourage, and in some cases require parents to be full partners in their children's schooling. Many parents report that teachers and principals make them feel at home in their children's schools and that school is a welcoming and not a threatening place. They have a sense that their children's teachers care not only about their children but about their entire family. This serves to foster a sense of shared goals, goals that in the case of Catholic schools are focused clearly on academic excellence (Bempechat, Drago-Severson, & Dindorff, 1994).

I do not believe that there is anything secretive or magical to this successful model of home–school connection. Public schools can do what Catholic schools have been doing. All it takes is the willingness to invest time and effort in getting to know the children and families that the school serves. Regrettably, where many public schools are concerned, this kind of investment of time and effort seems to be at a premium. I cannot pretend to know why. I can only argue from my vantage point that the payoff in children's psychological and academic well-being is worth it.

PRACTICE CULTURAL SENSITIVITY

The immediate consequence of these findings for teachers is that educational interventions need not necessarily be targeted differently to specific ethnic groups. All children need to believe in their ability to learn and master new skills. All children need to understand that effort does not necessarily imply lack of ability and that mistakes and failure are an essential part of the process of learning.

This does not mean, however, that we can happily ignore cultural differences in how parents choose to prepare their children for schooling, nor should we neglect to consider cultural differences in how children come to understand the reasons for success and failure. On the contrary, as the childhood population becomes increasingly diverse, we have to pay ever more attention to the ways in which children from different ethnic and cultural backgrounds come to understand the roles that effort and ability play in academic achievement. Susan Holloway (1988) has discussed the difficulties inherent in understanding achievement in families for whom concepts such as effort and ability mean such different things. In my earlier discussion of education in Japan and China, I noted the prevailing view that intelligence is a quality that always grows, given effort and diligence in the pursuit of knowledge. From an intellectual point of view, whatever level of education one attains, and the excellence with which one attains it, is a matter that is entirely within one's control. It is only lack of effort that can limit educational and career outcomes.

In contrast, Western views of intelligence rely very heavily on notions of innate ability and inheritability. Intelligence is a trait that one is born with, that cannot change very much, and that is not subject to individual control. By definition, then, intelligence is both *limited* and *limiting*. And so it is easy to see the difficulties faced by teachers and educational researchers. The very same terms, such as effort and ability, can mean very different things to members of different cultural groups. However, this should not keep us from understanding how children come to understand the role of effort and ability in their school performance. It can only help us in our quest to have all children realize their intellectual potential.

However, as Jimenez (Bempechat, et al., 1997) has argued, cultural sensitivity is not conveyed in the lowering of standards. For example, the fact that a child speaks a language other than English at home should in no way lead teachers to adopt a two-tiered system of learning, with higher standards for native English speakers and lower standards for immigrant children. Rather, cultural sensitivity—ever more necessary in our schools—is realized through a healthy balance between respecting the ways in which culture and ethnicity guide the academic and motivational support that parents provide for their children, and maintaining high academic goals for all children.

ENCOURAGE SCHOOL CHOICE

We have come a long way from the days when we believed that we needed to fix what was wrong with poor and minority families. Families do not need to be *fixed*—they need to be supported in their efforts to educate their children in ways they see fit. For many parents, this has recently come to mean the ability to choose the schools in which they want to see their children educated. Through school voucher programs, parents are able to use public funds that would have gone to their child's designated school to send their child to a school of their own choosing. The recent high court ruling in Wisconsin opened the door for parents to use public funds to send their children to parochial schools, thus eschewing constitutional concerns about the separation of church and state. In addition, the growing charter school movement allows communities to use government funds to create new schools which are unfettered by traditional public school bureaucracy.

Unfortunately, in the arena of public policy, one cannot avoid the criticism that to advocate school choice is to abandon the plight of inner-city public schools. The concerns are by now familiar. Officials worry that school choice options will, of necessity, siphon money from public school systems, which are increasingly in need of financial support. These kinds of school choice programs also have the potential to attract the best and most motivated students—the cream of the crop, if you will, leaving behind the least prepared and motivated students in schools ever more depleted of funds (Hill, et al., 1990).

I am not a public policy analyst. I do not think in terms of schools as entities; my concerns lie with parents and their children. From my place in this debate, school choice is a critical tool that helps educationally underserved children attain and even surpass their current intellectual potential. I am certainly not against public schooling. Yet we must be honest with ourselves and acknowledge that it is both unreasonable and unfair to expect parents to wait out school reform efforts until their neighborhood public school becomes an effective institution that can meet their children's intellectual and social needs. It is the height of hypocrisy for middle-class politicians to seek the best for their own children but advocate what in many cases is the worst for poor children. Poor parents are no different from middle-class parents; we need to help and not hinder them in their search for the best quality education they can find for their children.

8

"To Seek Mind Where It Is Mindful"

Educational researchers are at a crossroads. There is no question that we have a much deeper conceptual understanding of children's motivation to achieve in school than we once did. If we have learned anything over the past two decades of research and study, it is that children are very active participants in their learning. They are very attuned to the subtle messages that parents and teachers convey about schooling and learning, and they know—they *really* know—how we feel about their abilities to learn and master new skills. On the basis of what we parents and teachers manage to communicate about their abilities, children quickly learn to interpret our pity as a sign that we think they lack ability and our anger as a sign that we have high expectations for them and that they could and should do *much* better. The interpretations that children make become beliefs that influence the academic choices that children make when they learn and the persistence they show when they are engaged in learning.

Regrettably, the three kinds of research studies that have generated most of our knowledge are all quite limited in what they can tell us about what children actually *understand*. The first are experimental studies, in which we carefully manipulate children's beliefs about a new kind of problem and control as many factors as possible while they learn the problem. Bruner and Haste (1987) have suggested that this kind of research reflects the investigator's view of the "child as scientist." For example, I conducted a study in which I wanted to know if teachers could manipulate children's beliefs about an ability as being either changeable or fixed (Bempechat, et al., 1991). I divided one group of students into two smaller groups, and depending on which group each child was in, read a different set of instructions for a new kind of problem. One group received instructions that focused on the malleability of this skill, while the other group heard instructions that emphasized the innateness of the skill in question. Having accomplished this manipulation, I was then able to see if the two groups differed in their expectations for success, their confidence, and so on. I measured all these very interesting factors through scales and questionnaires. In retrospect, I am disappointed that I did not actually have a real conversation with these children. I would have learned so much more about how they felt about the problems once they began solving them. I could have asked them, for example, if they believed me when I told them that the skill was innate. I did not do this, though, because my method of inquiry was singularly focused on what Bruner and Haste (1987) call the "lone child." In doing so, I neglected to probe the social and cultural contexts in which these children were living and growing.

The second kind of investigations are survey studies, in which educational researchers ask children to relate how different kinds of learning experiences affect all manner of beliefs about learning, such as their beliefs about the causes of success and failure in the classroom, their confidence in their abilities, and their expectations for their school performance in the future. Third are survey studies in which the researchers manipulate details of hypothetical stories of success and failure. They ask children to predict how hypothetical children might react to such stories and describe what they think of the hypothetical children's abilities, of how hard they tried, and so on.

In and of themselves, these research strategies have not been bad or wrong; they have been limited. In no way do I wish to trivialize the collective efforts of the educational research community to which I have contributed and of which I am a part. Truthfully, though, we cannot know that one thousand children interpret the item "My parents make me feel ashamed if I do poorly in school" in the exact same way. No amount of pilot testing can assure us that this is the case. The concept of shame varies widely from culture to culture and from individual to individual.

Additionally, we must admit that it is of little sensible help for teachers to know how children respond to hypothetical stories about hypothetical children. Our nation's children are not hypothetical nor are they theoretical; they are real children in real families that struggle with daily life stressors, of which their children's schooling is but one. For all our efforts, we lack a genuine understanding of what these children make of their experiences in school, how they influence the ways in which they approach learning in their classrooms on a day-to-day basis, how the adults and peers in their lives influence their views of achievement and opportunity in our society, and how all these beliefs evolve over time. Educational researchers need to take advantage of children's growing realization that they do not so much act on the world as they act on their beliefs about the world. As our nation becomes increasingly diverse, our need to understand these issues becomes more urgent. We must begin to listen carefully to the voices of the children and parents we have been seeking to understand.

In other words, it is time that educational researchers adopted a different approach to their craft, one that integrates individual beliefs and attitudes about learning with cultural psychology and that focuses on how the cultures and contexts in which children grow influence the ways that they make sense of the world around them. Bronfenbrenner (1979), Bruner (1990), Haste (1987, 1993), and Cole (1996) have been arguing for some time now that individual thinking and understanding does not evolve independently of cultural and social environments. It is simply impossible to separate the individual from the context (Bronfenbrenner, 1979; Haste, 1987, 1993; Vygotsky, 1962, 1978).

How can we go about developing a deeper understanding of how children, parents, and teachers think about schooling and the factors that lead to success? I believe that we need to set aside momentarily—although not completely abandon—traditional quantitative methods of conducting educational research. By traditional quantitative methods, I am referring to the three kinds of studies I just mentioned, though they give us lots of data to analyze and statistics to report. Educational researchers need to do something more than this, something that most do not—they need to sit down and talk with children, parents, and teachers. These kinds of *qualitative* studies, based on carefully designed interviews, will give us the opportunity to learn firsthand how children and the adults in their lives actually think about schooling and the role that education plays in their lives.

Carefully designed interviews are composed of in-depth questions that are based on knowledge from previous research but have the advantage of allowing individuals to use their own words to describe their schooling experiences and the meanings that these experiences have for them. As Bronfenbrenner (1979), Shweder (1991), and others have argued, the chance to talk openly about experiences leads us to a better understanding of the cultures and contexts in which children, parents, and teachers live and work. Thus where I have previously asked children to rank in order reasons that *I* provide for success and failure, I would now ask children to talk to me about an incident in which they succeeded or failed, how this made them feel about their abilities, how it affected their confidence, and how it made them think about the particular subject area.

Despite our collective research endeavors, we do indeed lack a contextualized, theoretically grounded picture of what makes some students excel where so many others falter. For example, many researchers have found that parents who have high expectations for their children's grades in school have children who tend to do better in school than children of parents who have rather low expectations for their performance. Interviews would give us the opportunity to understand how children interpret these expectations.

Recall that our studies found that parent involvement was negatively associated with math achievement. Parents who were perceived as providing frequent academic and motivational support had children who tended to do poorly in math. Knowing this, it would be interesting to know how these students interpret their parents' involvement. Some may think that their parents believe that they are stupid in math. Some may believe that they would be better off without what they perceive as relentless nagging.

What about the higher-achieving students? Their performance in math was associated with a lesser tendency on the part of their parents to provide academic and motivational support. Conceivably, some students may be very happy with this hands-off approach. Others may crave a little more attention to their schoolwork than they are receiving. For teachers who struggle to convey their concerns about a particular child's progress, this kind of knowledge would be enormously helpful in building the home–school connections of which I spoke in Chapter Seven. What is patently clear to me, at the end of this phase of my research on families and schooling, is that the Educational Socialization Scale can provide none of this rich and compelling information.

At the same time, we certainly do not want to completely abandon traditional, quantitative educational research. It has important advantages, not the least of which is the ability to allow us to make assumptions about larger groups of students. As a case in point, there is no doubting the wealth of information we have gained from large-scale surveys about the higher achievement of minority students in Catholic as compared to public schools. As I have discussed, there is ample debate about the interpretation of the accumulated findings. Are Catholic school students more motivated to begin with? Are their parents more concerned about and involved in their children's education? Simply put, are these comparisons inherently unfair?

Carefully crafted interviews, built on the knowledge we have accumulated from the existing literature, would yield a much greater understanding of how ethnic minority students benefit from Catholic schooling. This kind of research would help us develop a deeper understanding than we currently have of how parents and children go about their choice of Catholic school and what teachers think about why parents make these choices. Qualitative studies would allow us to examine how individual teachers, students, and parents make sense of their Catholic school experiences and enhance our knowledge of the ways in which these schools influence children's learning and motivation. For example, how do teachers think about aspects of their teaching that encourage students to acquire adaptive beliefs about learning? How do individual minority students reason about the relationship between education and opportunity in our society? For instance, it would be very interesting to learn that, as a group, African American students in Catholic schools speak more often than those in public schools about the essential tie between a strong education and a successful future.

Further, open-ended in-depth interviews with parents, teachers, and students about various elements of the academic experience might reveal that what teachers feel to be essential elements in their practice differs from what parents or students perceive to be essential elements (Bempechat & Drago-Severson, 1998). It would probably also be the case that within each group, individuals would have different perspectives on what matters most to them. For example, what matters most to African American students and the ways that they talk about *how* it matters are likely to differ. Indeed, qualitative research has the capacity to challenge long-held assumptions about cross-ethnic and cross-cultural achievement. In my work, it has helped to address the either/or paradigm that has permeated scholarship in our field. I present two studies to illustrate this point.

CHALLENGING THE
EITHER/OR PARADIGM

Dependence on questionnaires, surveys, and experimental studies has led researchers to embrace an either/or approach to characterizing children's motivation to achieve. We all fully understand that the phenomena we are interested in do not manifest themselves as dichotomies but rather along continua. Yet much of our work lends itself to conclusions, for example, that children are either "entity" or "incremental" theorists (Dweck & Bempechat, 1983), that they are either "task" or "ego" involved (Nicholls, 1989), that they are either intrinsically or extrinsically motivated, or that they are oriented to "performance" or "learning" goals (Dweck & Bempechat, 1983). These characterizations make for cleaner, less encumbered studies and are intuitively appealing. However, they make little real-world sense. All of us can recognize at one or another time that we simultaneously believe in aspects of these dichotomous views.

Take the notion that children believe *either* in the stability of ability (entity theorist) *or* the malleability of ability (incremental theorist); this dichotomy simply does not ring true when explored in any depth. Anderson (1995) has argued that the fact that these theories can be so easily manipulated suggests that individuals can simultaneously hold the "knowledge structures" inherent in both entity and incremental theories but choose to make use of one or the other structure in a given situation. Alternatively, individuals are probably able to believe simultaneously in aspects of both theories and make use of both of them at the same time. To illustrate, it does not make sense that children who are categorized as incremental theorists are committed to learning no matter the cost to their performance in school. It is more reasonably the case that incremental theorists want to expand their skills and knowledge but are also conscious of the need to do well in school. Similarly, it is more likely that entity theorists want to increase their competence while at the same time maintaining a level of achievement with which they feel comfortable.

As a first step in exploring this puzzle, my colleagues and I were interested in knowing the degree to which children's categorizations as entity or incremental theorists would mesh with their views in an interview setting (Quihuis & Bempechat, 1997). Quihuis designed a study in which we asked poor Mexican American high school students (all of whom were English proficient) to complete Dweck's theories of intelligence questionnaire; we then interviewed a subsample of the students. The questionnaire was focused not only on their beliefs about their abilities in general but also in the specific domains of mathematics, science, and social studies.

We found that all students who endorsed an incremental theory, no matter the domain, spoke very passionately about the degree to which their abilities can grow, provided that effort was sustained. Our most interesting and unexpected finding, though, concerned the entity theorists, who spoke initially of their beliefs with the characteristic uncertainty and low confidence associated with a view that sees ability as limited and limiting. Yet when asked to elaborate on their beliefs, they asserted positions that were consistent with incremental theory, articulating the kinds of mastery-oriented strategies ordinarily associated with incremental beliefs. For example, one student acknowledged that she was dumb in math, that it had never come easily to her, and that she did not do well. She then offered that if she needed to fulfill a math requirement to gain entry into post high school studies, she would "break her head" to do well by hiring a tutor and doing extra work. This is the kind of strategic thinking ordinarily associated with an incremental theory.

This finding poses a serious challenge to Dweck's theory. It seems that when confidence is low, entity theorists are able to articulate effective strategies for achieving success, particularly when the need to perform well is high. Thus using a different methodology allowed us to demonstrate that the same individual can hold different theories in the same domain, as speculated by Lewis (1995). It is possible that our qualitative methodology revealed what Darley (1995) refers to as the "optimistic entity theorist." That is, despite what may be a record of relatively poor performance, these students believe that they have the ability to succeed in a domain in which they have experienced difficulty. These students could be simultaneously holding aspects of the knowledge structures inherent in both theories, as elaborated by Anderson (1995; see also Schunk, 1995). This suggests that entity theorists with low confidence may indeed be capable of demonstrating mastery-oriented strategies in the face of challenge, much like their incremental counterparts. How effectively they may be able to do this is open to question, as we did not study students' actual behaviors in an achievement situation.

What does all this imply? My view is that, for entity theorists, achievement beliefs expressed in a decontextualized experimental setting are likely to vary considerably from those asserted in an interview designed to elicit the *meanings* students attach to their beliefs. As Jimenez has noted (Quihuis, Bempechat, & Jimenez, 1998), responding to interview questions allowed these students to place their beliefs in the context of day-to-day learning in which a variety of social factors such as teacher expectations and peer influence, structural factors such as tracking, and internal factors such as the value placed on a given subject are likely to play a role in their achievement views.

Indeed, the prototypical experimental study puts the researcher in the position of imposing abstract categories on what students understand to be true for them. Much of our knowledge derives from *etic* concepts—categories that researchers force onto children's ideas, such as "entity" and "incremental." This reliance on artificial concepts moves us further and further away from the meanings that children construct about their learning experiences. We know so little about students' *emic* concepts of intelligence—those idiosyncratic and contextualized perspectives, bound by standards defined by students themselves. When documenting the varieties of intelligence, Howard Gardner (1983) argued that the exclusive use of surveys to assess children's notions of their own intelligence deprives us of the opportunity to capitalize on what they perceive as their own intellectual strengths and weaknesses. In this regard, it is very interesting that John Nicholls (1990) believes that it is not particularly helpful for researchers to focus on how students perceive or conceptualize ability. According to Nicholls, researchers should focus their efforts on exploring the *meanings* that students attach to their work (see also Holloway, 1988). Rather than asking how children judge ability, Nicholls argues that much richer information can be gleaned from asking children what they think ability is—its underlying meanings—and how these differ as a function of student characteristics such as age, ethnicity, and social class. He cautions that we need to be careful not to project our own conceptions of ability onto children. Regrettably, the trend in our field has been to do just this; we need to give serious consideration to children's meaning making around issues of their school achievement.

CHALLENGING NEGATIVE ASSUMPTIONS IN POST-APARTHEID SOUTH AFRICA

Recent political developments in South Africa coincided with an opportunity to spend time with adolescents who grew up under conditions of apartheid but now find themselves members of a newly democratic society (Bempechat & Abrahams, 1998). This study grew out of a research project on adolescents' conceptions of justice and morality under apartheid (Abrahams, 1995). The interviews were conducted by Salie Abrahams, a black South African who was born in Cape Town, where he served as a community worker, educator, and researcher, and was actively involved in the struggle against apartheid. This placed us, as researchers, in a unique position to examine how these students make meaning in the context of political and social change.

Unarguably, most black children in South Africa have been subjected to extreme and officially sanctioned institutionalized apartheid, expressed, among other ways, in consistently underfunded schools with few or very poor facilities and very little or no chance for educational advancement and career opportunity (Abrahams, 1995). Recent estimates show that prior to 1994 the government typically expended at least ten times more for the education of white as compared to black children (Abrahams, 1988). Educational disadvantage is but one way in which the culture of apartheid had created a hostile environment that threatened healthy psychosocial development.

According to achievement motivation theory, this history might lead one to expect black children to develop beliefs and behaviors about achievement that were maladaptive for learning (Weiner, 1985; see Dweck & Bempechat, 1983). For example, the literature on teacher expectancy effects, of which we spoke earlier, has shown that teachers who base their opinions of children's intellectual ability largely on external characteristics such as race or social class act on their beliefs in ways that indirectly influence children's performance in the classroom. This self-fulfilling prophecy is particularly pervasive in teachers whose negative beliefs are consistent and rigidly held (Rosenthal, 1995; Rosenthal & Jacobson, 1968).

John Ogbu's (1986) work on achievement among African American students has shown that the experience of racism and prejudice leads some students to develop an oppositional approach to education. For example, Fordham and Ogbu (1986) argue that African American students, being members of a caste-like minority, do poorly in school because they experience "inordinate ambivalence and affective dissonance" regarding academic success. That is, because whites historically refused to acknowledge black intellectual ability, blacks began to doubt their abilities and view achievement as the province of whites only. Fordham and Ogbu also argue that blacks have developed an "oppositional frame of reference," documenting ways in which peers actively discourage one another from doing well in school on the grounds that such behavior is considered "acting white" in the American context.

While there may be comparabilities between African Americans in the United States and South African blacks, of course there are enormous differences between these two social contexts. African Americans are a minority in a white culture but are officially equal; opportunities for achievement exist in a context in which institutional barriers are more subtle. Notwithstanding these concerns, it is possible that some parallels may exist in the achievement experiences of black students in these two cultures.

However, to assume negative outcomes for all children who grow up under extreme circumstances is problematic. We do know that under such conditions some children emerge seemingly psychologically intact, having developed effective coping mechanisms (Garmezy, 1993; Garmezy & Neuchterlein, 1972; Rutter, 1987). Researchers have documented a variety of protective factors that appear to serve as buffers against psychological risks such as apartheid. These mitigating factors include self-understanding, or the tendency to reflect on oneself and the events in one's life, *as well as* taking thoughtful action consistent with one's reflections; close relationships with adults and peers with whom one can share thoughts, feelings, and experiences; role models who are supportive; and dedication to a cause (Beardslee, 1990; Cohler, 1987; Garmezy and Masten, 1990; Kimchi & Schaffner, 1990; Werner & Smith, 1989).

Interestingly, in the South African context, schools throughout the eighties became important sites of the struggle against apartheid. Many black students used schools as a place where they demonstrated their collective action (through "stayaways," economic boycotts, and defiance campaigns). Whereas schools had been used as instruments of dispossession by the state, they were "repossessed" by students and became instruments of both political and psychological empowerment (Bloch, 1988; Bundy, 1985). It is possible, then, that students who were involved in the struggle, by virtue of their active participation, have developed adaptive beliefs about their personal efficacy. For some students, individual resiliency may well have been facilitated by their social context. We make no distinction here between individuals and their social context (Bronfenbrenner, 1979).

Our purpose was to examine the achievement beliefs of adolescents who grew up under apartheid and to explore the ways in which they negotiate the meaning of opportunity in the new, post-apartheid South Africa. We specifically explored students' beliefs about achievement and schooling and probed the ways in which they talk about the relationship between education and the future. We integrated the social cognitive approach to achievement motivation, with its focus on beliefs about learning (attributions for success and failure) with cultural psychology, which focuses on culture and context as central constructs in the development of meaning making. Rather than distribute questionnaires, we tried to extend our understanding of achievement motivation by focusing on achievement cognitions *in context*. In keeping with our own evolving views of our field, we recognized that cognitive processes and factors in the cultural and social environment are not independent; as noted scholars have argued, one cannot separate the individual from the context (Bronfenbrenner, 1979; Haste, 1993; Vygotsky, 1978). Given our purpose, it was important that we be guided by theory that incorporates both individual cognition and an appreciation of the social and cultural context.

Thus our methods were based on the theoretical work of Vygotsky (1962, 1978), which has been expanded by Helen Haste (1993; Bruner & Haste, 1987) and Barbara Rogoff (1990). Vygotsky argues that the cultural and historical context of individuals play a significant role in guiding the development of their belief systems. Haste argues that, if we take Vygotsky seriously, then we must acknowledge that individual meaning making is influenced not only by the cultural and social-historical context but by the social interactions through which meaning is negotiated, as well as the individual's cognitive capacity.

In her interpretation of Vygotsky's work, Rogoff (1990) argues that the culture—and its institutions such as schools and economic and political systems—shapes our thinking and provides the values and the standards for our thinking. In the process of development we are always subject to the social and environmental context that fashions our reasoning. Rogoff finds that there appear to be local relationships between school practices and specific cognitive activities (Rogoff, 1990).

Thus according to Rogoff, the cultural context shapes children's thinking and ultimately plays a crucial role in determining the content as well as the nature of meaning making. Rogoff further argues that the social context should not be seen as influencing or not influencing development. The social context, from her perspective, is part of the developing child at all times, and context cannot be separated from meaning making (see also Shweder, 1991).

Over a series of three extensive, open-ended individual interviews, we asked 11 sixteen- and seventeen-year-old students to talk to us about their schooling experiences, their friends, and the influential adults in their lives, and to reflect on the events they had lived through and were currently experiencing. We examined students' comments through the theoretical lens of what Haste has referred to as the "Vygotsky triangle," which takes into account not only *intraindividual* cognitive capacities, but also the *interindividual* and *cultural contexts* in which beliefs evolve and meaning making takes place. How did these students make sense of their experiences? How did the beliefs of those around them influence their developing ideas? What impact did apartheid have on their formative years, and how did they imagine their lives in a post-apartheid society?

What emerged were clearly articulated beliefs around three main themes—education, opportunity, and the future. Our approach to meaning making allowed us to see the ways in which, despite the extreme conditions of prejudice and oppression, the South African adolescents in our study showed remarkable resilience, personal efficacy, and sense of purpose.

From an *intrapersonal* perspective, we saw that, despite having come of age in a system that was designed to oppress, the adolescents in our study maintained a very positive outlook on education, opportunities, and their futures. While these students shared a set of cultural beliefs about the history of apartheid, hard work, persistence, and the like, they owned certain beliefs—that is, they affirmed them as their own and as being a powerful source of motivation. They told stories and articulated answers in which they communicated a clearly integrated worldview that related to their own identity and their ideas about education, opportunity, and the future. Their involvement in the struggle against apartheid and their bitterness over past injustices seemed to have given them a sense of purpose and strengthened their resolve to better their lives and the lives of those around them. Despite their personal knowledge that their schools were at a severe disadvantage relative to schools in white areas, these students generally spoke positively of their learning experiences, their teachers, and their schools. Their descriptions of their individual meaning making about their approaches to learning and education highlighted a strong sense of hard work, determination, and persistence, not only in their day-to-day schoolwork but also in the pursuit of long-term personal goals.

These students not only learned to live through the severe deprivation that apartheid produced, but also adopted the delay of gratification as a way of life. None wanted to drop out of school to take jobs (although money in the home was sorely needed). They all recognized that the short-term gain would be quickly outweighed by the long-term loss. For the young women, their personal resolve to better themselves emerged in the context of their opposition to early and unwanted pregnancy. All were clear that such an occurrence would result in early school departure and would most likely derail their educational and career futures. Indeed, this would place them on a negative trajectory from which it would be difficult if not impossible to rebound.

From an *interpersonal* perspective, we found that the negotiation of meaning was expressed both explicitly and implicitly. Clearly, it was influenced by ongoing and *explicit* negotiations with family members, teachers, and peers. In addition, those who had struggled against apartheid provided these students with an *implicit* understanding of both the pragmatic and affective consequences of apartheid on their education, opportunities, and futures. The implicit meaning of this collective experience seemed to give rise to what sacrifice, persistence, determination, and hard work entailed. Further, the students seemed to be embracing for themselves the lessons they had gleaned from the people in their lives—that success in any endeavor will ultimately result from sacrifice, hard work, and resilience, even in the face of major obstacles. Through their ongoing interpersonal negotiations, it became clear to these students that the journey from educational disadvantage to intellectual fulfillment and self-actualization would not be an easy one.

The young women negotiated explicitly their meaning making about early pregnancy with their teachers, mothers, and peers. It became clear, however, that peers were the most influential group with whom they implicitly negotiated their understanding of the consequences; friends supported one another in their determination to avoid early and unwanted pregnancy.

The students shared common beliefs about opportunity and education that appeared to operate at three levels—past, present, and future. Clearly, the unique timing of our investigation made this possible. The students often described, in remarkably similar ways, their bitterness over past inequalities of educational and career opportunity, their present determination to seize the opportunities that were newly available to them, and their strategies for achieving their future goals. Their commitment to become highly educated and to delay gratification in the pursuit of this objective was embedded in the culture of the struggle.

From a *social-historical* or cultural perspective, it is important to underscore the singular timing of our investigation. The students in our study were entering young adulthood with unprecedented promises of educational and career opportunities. In a sense, the struggle against apartheid became their cultural inheritance and a cultural resource available to them for meaning making. Indeed, these students were born into a culture of protest that evolved into a culture of promise, in which they could, with optimism, look forward to a future society burgeoning with equal educational opportunity. Their present notions of optimism operated at two levels. A long-term optimism, sparked by the election of the African National Congress, appeared to go hand in hand with a short-term realism, fostered by unchanged day-to-day living conditions.

The students seemed to understand, however, that while the systemic obstacles have been officially eliminated, they still face the psychological obstacles that are the legacy of apartheid. This is reflected in their notion of "apartheid in the mind." As one student explained: "Some people still have apartheid in their minds. We will have to teach the whites that they are not superior, that it is not so. But we will also have to teach ourselves that apartheid was a stupid idea and that you can't oppress yourself."

Imagine, for a moment, how our interpretations of our findings would have been limited by the parameters imposed by traditional achievement motivation theory. Relying exclusively on attribution theory (as in Weiner, 1985) or goal theory (as in Bempechat et al., 1991; Nicholls, 1989), it would not be unreasonable to expect that black South African students might be justifiably contemptuous of an institution (the school) that set so many hurdles in their path to intellectual attainment. Instead, we found that these students held their contempt not for the school as an institution, but rather for those who engineered such a blatantly racist system of education. As an institution, the school was seen as the only path to advancement—a path that had to be embraced to achieve success and black progress.

We would have been on sure psychological ground in predicting a myriad of motivational factors that have been shown to hinder academic achievement, such as low confidence, low expectations for learning, and low aspirations for the future, all of which are associated with the tendency to succumb to learned helplessness in the classroom. On the contrary, however, our findings suggest that these South African students, born into the culture of apartheid, developed adaptive survival strategies reflected in their resilience in the face of hardship and their determination to overcome obstacles. Their individual meaning making around issues of schooling and opportunity, negotiated in the social setting and the cultural context, reveals a strong self-perception of ability and a deep commitment to personal sacrifice in the pursuit of long-term goals. How did these evolve? To be sure, we cannot know the degree to which the students' adaptive approach to life was fostered by individual temperamental characteristics, the school, the family, the peer group, or the social-historical context. It would be highly problematic, however, to attribute students' meaning making to one or more factors and exclude the others. In keeping with our integrative approach, we believe it is most likely a combination of all these factors.

Further, these factors are representative of those protective buffers described by scholars of risk and resiliency. The students' descriptions of their coping strategies demonstrate self-understanding as defined by Beardslee (1990)—that inner reflection on themselves and events in their lives, coupled with measured actions of protest that were consistent with their reflections. Their meaning making was supported by strong interpersonal relations with peers and adults (Garmezy & Masten, 1990). In addition, they had strong role models (see Kimchi & Schaffner, 1990) who were supportive of their actions and to whom they could look for strength and guidance—primarily their mothers and Nelson Mandela.

The Vygotsky triangle (Haste, 1993), then, provided us with new ways of understanding the influence of motivational factors in learning and achievement. We were able to show that at the meeting point of social cognition and cultural psychology lies a deeper appreciation of the ways in which students conceptualize schooling and achievement. By taking into account individual cognitions, the social setting, and the cultural context in which children develop, we shed greater light on but adolescent meaning making. This approach has allowed us to see the ways in which, despite the extreme conditions of prejudice and oppression, the South African adolescents in our study showed remarkable resilience, personal efficacy, and sense of purpose.

MOVING OUR UNDERSTANDINGS FORWARD

Parents, teachers, and researchers have struggled for decades to understand the puzzle of differential achievement and motivation in ethnic America, and more recently, across cultures. I believe that we shall be able to put these pieces together only to the degree that we are able to combine quantitative and qualitative methodologies, and etic and emic approaches to understanding the cultures and contexts in which meanings are created and communicated.

Resonating with this view, Shweder (1990) argues that researchers must attend to the ways in which cultural conceptions of self and society are organized and operate in the day-to-day life of individuals: "the mind . . . is content-driven, domain-specific, and constructively stimulus-bound; and it cannot be extracted from the historically variable and cross-culturally diverse intentional worlds in which it plays a coconstituting part. . . . It is the aim of cultural psychology to understand the organization and evocative power of all that stuff, to study the major varieties of it, and *to seek mind where it is mindful*, indissociably embedded in the meaning and resources that are its product, yet also make it up" (italics added, p. 13).

In this connection, Sigel and his colleagues (Sigel, 1992; Sigel, McGillicuddy-DeLisi, & Goodnow, 1992) note the tendency of researchers to rely on methods of data collection such as questionnaires and surveys: "The use of such traditional methodologies prompts us to wonder whether respondents, given the opportunity to give free-floating and far-reaching narratives, might conceivably structure the topic quite differently and add dimensions not antic-ipated by the researcher" (p. xv).

There is undoubtedly some truth to Sigel's observation. I am not proposing the abandonment of traditional quantitative methods, but rather the addition of qualitative "free-floating and far-reaching narratives"; both methodologies are vital to our ability to extend knowledge. Used in combination, both methods can help us build grounded theory. The more we understand the mechanisms that account for academic success in poor and minority children, the greater our chances of helping all children to excel in school. This knowledge is well within our grasp. When we begin in earnest to build a more meaningful knowledge base, we will then become of real help to teachers and parents. We can progress toward this goal by integrating achievement motivation theory, with its focus on achievement-related cognitions, with principles that have emerged in cultural psychology. This means an open acknowledgment of the centrality of meaning making in context. Future research in our field must incorporate both individual meaning making and an appreciation of the social and cultural contexts in which children learn and grow.

Appendix

. . . .

The research reported in this book made use of two questionnaires, the Sydney Attribution Scale (Math Section), developed by Herbert Marsh and his colleagues (Marsh et al., 1984), and the Educational Socialization Scale, developed by Bempechat and her colleagues (Bempechat, Mordkowitz, Wu, Morison, & Ginsburg, 1989). Each scale is reproduced below.

SYDNEY ATTRIBUTION SCALE*

In responding to the scale, each child indicates the degree of agreement or disagreement with **each** of the three possible explanations on a scale of 1 (false) to 5 (true).

1. Suppose you have to swap books with someone to correct some math problems and no one wants to give you their book. This is probably because . . .

   a. nobody likes you very much.
   b. you are careless in your work and with corrections.
   c. everyone knows you do math badly.

---

*© 1984 by Herbert Marsh. Used by permission. Not to be reproduced without permission of Herbert Marsh.

2. Suppose the teacher wanted you to help correct some math tests. This is probably because . . .

   a. you are one of the best students in math.
   b. it was your turn to do it.
   c. you always try to do well at math.

3. Suppose you got a math question wrong in class. It is probably because . . .

   a. you often have trouble in math.
   b. the question was hard.
   c. you never pay attention in math classes.

4. Suppose you are chosen from your school to take part in a state math competition. This is probably because . . .

   a. you will try your best.
   b. you were lucky.
   c. you are good at math.

5. Suppose the class was asked to choose the best five people in math. If they chose you it would be because . . .

   a. you really are one of the best at math.
   b. you worked hard to be good at math.
   c. they like you.

6. Suppose you get a math problem to do on the board in front of the class and you do it wrong. This is probably because . . .

   a. you are unlucky to be asked the hardest problem.
   b. you always have trouble solving problems.
   c. you did it too quickly and made a silly mistake.

7. Suppose the teacher shows you a new way of doing something in math and you get it wrong. This is probably because . . .

   a. you should pay more attention.
   b. the teacher explains things badly.
   c. anything in math is hard for you.

8. Suppose the teacher tells you not to help a friend with their math. This would probably be because . . .

    a. you should work harder on your own math.
    b. you make a lot of mistakes in math yourself.
    c. it is unfair.

9. Suppose the teacher asks you to collect and count the money for a class trip. It would probably be because . . .

    a. it is your turn to collect money this time.
    b. you always try hard in math classes.
    c. you are good at math and will collect the right money.

10. Suppose you did badly on a math test. This is probably because . . .

    a. you always do badly on math tests.
    b. you spend too little time studying math.
    c. the test was hard for everyone.

11. Suppose the teacher chooses you to do a special problem in math. It would probably be because . . .

    a. you know more than most children.
    b. you would work harder on it than your classmates.
    c. nobody else wanted to do it.

Educational Socialization Scale

Factor	Items	Cronbach's α	N
Future	My parents talk about different kinds of jobs I can have when I grow up. My parents say it's important to think about what I want to be in the future. My parents say it's important to think about the kinds of things I'm interested in doing when I grow up. My parents say it's important to think about what I want to be when I grow up.	.81	595
Teaching	My parents (or someone else at home) help me with math homework My parents (or someone else at home) help me with homework (not math). My parents give me math problems that the teacher hasn't taught yet.	.72	595
Effort	My parents say I could do better in school if I worked harder. My parents say you can get smarter and smarter as long as you try hard. My parents say if I don't do well on a test, it's probably because I didn't study hard enough or long enough. My parents say I can get good grades in school as long as I always try hard.	.76	595
Shame	My parents make me feel ashamed if I do badly in school. I feel ashamed if I do badly in school. My parents feel ashamed if I do badly in school. My parents punish me when I don't do well in school.	.73	595
Guilt	I feel badly because my parents work so hard to give me a good education. I feel badly that my parents have to work so hard.	.65	595

Cronbach's α is a measure of the reliability of each subscale that makes up the ESS. N is the number of respondents who answered the questions that make up each subscale.

Suggestions for Further Reading

• •

Details of the research reported in this book are available in the following reports publications:

Bempechat, J. (1992). The intergenerational transfer of motivational skills. In T. Sticht, M. Beeler, & B. McDonald (Eds.), *The intergenerational transfer of cognitive skills, Vol. II*, pp. 41–48. Norwood, NJ: Ablex.

Bempechat, J., & Abrahams, S. (1998). "You can't oppress yourself": Negotiating the meaning of opportunity in post-apartheid South Africa. Manuscript submitted for publication.

Bempechat, J., & Drago-Severson, E. (1998). *Attributions for success and failure: A comparative study of Catholic and public school students.* Unpublished manuscript, Harvard University.

Bempechat, J., Drago-Severson, E., & Dindorff, L. (1994, February/March). Parents assess Catholic schools. *Momentum*, pp. 57–61.

Bempechat, J., Graham, S., & Jimenez, N. (in press). The socialization of achievement in poor and minority children: A comparative study. *Journal of Cross-Cultural Psychology.*

Bempechat, J., Jimenez, N., & Graham, S. (1997). Motivational influences in the achievement of poor and minority children. *Journal of Child and Youth Care Work, 11,* 48–60.

Bempechat, J., London, P., & Dweck, C. (1991). Conceptions of ability in major domains: An interview and experimental study. *Child Study Journal, 21,* 11–36.

Bempechat, J., Nakkula, M., & Ginsburg, H. (1996). Attributions as predictors of mathematics achievement: A comparative study. *Journal of Research and Development in Education, 29,* 53–59.

Bempechat, J., & Omori, M. (1990). Meeting the needs of Southeast Asian children. *Digest on Urban and Minority Education*, #68. New York: ERIC Clearinghouse on Urban Education.

Choi, Y. E., Bempechat, J., & Ginsburg, H. (1994). Educational socialization in Korean American children: A longitudinal study. *Journal of Applied Developmental Psychology, 15*, 313–318.

Dweck, C., & Bempechat, J. (1983). Children's theories of intelligence: Consequences for learning. In S. G. Paris, G. M. Olson & H. W. Stevenson (Eds.), *Learning and motivation in the classroom*. Hillsdale, NJ: Erlbaum.

Ginsburg, H., Bempechat, J., & Chung, Y. E. (1992). Parent influences on children's mathematics. In T. Sticht, M. Beeler, & B. McDonald (Eds.), *The intergenerational transfer of cognitive skills, Vol. II*, 91–121. Norwood, NJ: Ablex.

References

Abrahams, S. (1988). *Education in the eighties: Proceedings of the Kenton Conference*. Cape Town, South Africa: Kenton Organizing Committee, University of Cape Town Press.

Abrahams, S. (1995). *Moral reasoning in context: The construction of the adolescent moral world under apartheid*. Unpublished dissertation, Harvard University.

Anderson, C. (1995). Implicit theories in broad perspective. *Psychological Inquiry, 6,* 286–290.

Anson, R. (1987). *Best intentions: The education and killing of Edmund Perry*. New York: Random House.

Barker, G. & Graham, S. (1987). Developmental study of praise and blame as attributional cues. *Journal of Educational Psychology, 79,* 62–67.

Beardslee, W. (1990). Stress from parental depression: Child risk, self-understanding, and a preventive intervention. In L. E. Arnold (Ed.), *Childhood stress* (pp. 351–371). New York: Wiley.

Beaton, A., Mullis, I., Martin, M., Gonzalez, E., Kelly, D., & Smith, T. (1996). *Mathematics achievement in the middle school years: IEA's Third International Mathematics and Science Study*. Boston: Center for the Study of Testing, Evaluation, and Educational Policy, Boston College.

Bempechat, J., & Abrahams, S. (1998). "You can't oppress yourself": Negotiating the meaning of opportunity in post-apartheid South Africa. Manuscript submitted for publication.

Bempechat, J., & Drago-Severson, E. (1998). *Attributions for success and failure: A comparative study of Catholic and public school students*. Manuscript submitted for publication.

Bempechat, J., Drago-Severson, E., & Dindorff, L. (1994, February/March). Parents assess Catholic schools. *Momentum*, pp. 57–61.

Bempechat, J., Jimenez, N., & Graham, S. (1997). Motivational factors in learning: Implications for poor and minority children and youth. *Journal of Child and Youth Care Work, 11*, 48–60.

Bempechat, J., London, P., & Dweck, C. (1991). Children's conceptions of ability in major domains: An interview and experimental study. *Child Study Journal, 21*, 11–36.

Bempechat, J., Mordkowitz, E., Wu, J., Morison, M., & Ginsburg, H. (1989, April). *Achievement motivation in Cambodian refugee children: A comparative study*. Paper presented at the biennial meeting of the Society for Research in Child Development, Kansas City.

Bempechat, J., & Williams, D. (1995). *Parental influences on achievement cognition: The development of a parental educational socialization measure*. Unpublished manuscript, Harvard University.

Bernal, M., Saenz, D., & Knight, G. (1995). Ethnic identity and adaptation of Mexican American youths in school settings. In A. Padilla (Ed.), *Hispanic psychology: Critical issues in theory and research* (pp. 71–88). London: Sage.

Bloch, G. (1988). Organization as education: The struggle in Western Cape Schools 1986–1988. In S. Abrahams (Ed.), *Education in the eighties: Proceedings of the Kenton Conference*. Cape Town, South Africa: Kenton Organizing Committee, University of Cape Town Press.

Boardman, S., Harrington, C., & Horowitz, S. (1987). Successful women: A psychological investigation of family, class, and education origins. In B. Gutek & L. Larwood (Eds.), *Women's career development*. Newbury Park, CA: Sage.

Bronfenbrenner, U. (1979). *The ecology of human development*. Cambridge, MA: Harvard University Press.

Bruner, J. (1990). *Acts of meaning*. Cambridge, MA: Harvard University Press.

Bruner, J., & Haste, H. (Eds.). (1987). *Making sense: The child's construction of the world*. London: Methuen.

Bryk, A., Lee, V., & Holland, P. (1993). *Catholic schools and the common good*. Cambridge, MA: Harvard University Press.

Bundy, C. (1985). *Street sociology and pavement politics: Aspects of youth/student resistance in Cape Town*. Witwatersrand History Workshop: Witwatersrand University.

Caplan, N., Choy, M., & Whitmore, J. (1992, February). Indochinese refugee families and academic achievement. *Scientific American*, pp. 18–24.

Carey, L. (1991). *Black ice*. New York: Knopf.

Chall, J., Conard, S., & Harris-Sharples, S. (1991). *Should textbooks challenge students? The case for easier or harder textbooks*. New York: Teachers College Press.

Chao, R. (1996). Chinese and European American mothers' beliefs in the role of parenting in children's school success. *Journal of Cross-Cultural Psychology, 27*, 403–423.

Chen, C., & Stevenson, H. (1990). Homework: A cross-cultural comparison. *Child Development, 60*, 551–561.

Choi, Y. E., Bempechat, J., & Ginsburg, H. (1994). Educational socialization in Korean American children: A longitudinal study. *Journal of Applied Developmental Psychology, 15*, 313–318.

Clark, R. (1983). *Family life and school achievement: Why poor black children succeed and fail*. Chicago: University of Chicago Press.

Cobb, P., Wood, T., Yackel, E., Nicholls, J., Wheatley, G., Trigatti, B., & Perlwitz, M. (1991). Assessment of a problem-centered second-grade mathematics project. *Journal for Research in Mathematics Education, 22*, 3–29.

Cobb, P., Yackel, E., & Wood, T. (1992). A constructivist alternative to the representational view of mind in mathematics education. *Journal for Research in Mathematics Education, 23*, 2–33.

Cohler, B. (1987). Adversity, resilience, and the study of lives. In E. Anthony & J. Cohler (Eds.), *The invulnerable child*. New York: Guilford Press.

Cole, M. (1996). *Cultural psychology: A once and future discipline*. Cambridge, MA: Harvard University Press.

Coleman, J., & Hoffer, T. (1987). *Public and private high schools: The impact of communities*. New York: Basic Books.

Coleman, J., Hoffer, T., & Kilgore, S. (1987). Cognitive outcomes in public and private schools. *Sociology of Education, 55*, 65–76.

Comer, J. (1980). *School power: Implications of an intervention project*. New York: Free Press.

Covington, M., & Omelich, C. (1979). Effort: The double-edged sword in school achievement. *Journal of Educational Psychology, 71*, 169–182.

Darley, J. (1995). Mutable theories that organize the world. *Psychological Inquiry, 6*, 290–293.

Delgado-Gaitan, C. (1992). School matters in the Mexican American home: Socializing children to education. *American Educational Research Journal, 29*, 495–513.

Delgado-Gaitan, C. (1994). Consejos: The power of cultural narratives. *Anthropology and Education Quarterly, 25*, 298–316.

Delpit, L. (1996). Act your age, not your color. In J. Irvine and M. Foster (Eds.), *Growing up African-American in Catholic schools* (pp. 116–125). New York: Teachers College Press.

DeVos, G. (1978). Selective permeability and reference group sanctioning: Psychological continuities in role degradation. In J. Yinger & S. Cutler (Eds.), *Competing models of multiethnic and multiracial societies* (pp. 7–24). New York: American Sociological Association.

Diener, C. & Dweck, C. (1978). An analysis of learned helplessness: Continuous changes in performance, strategy, and achievement cognitions following failure. *Journal of Personality and Social Psychology, 36*, 451-462.

Diener, C. & Dweck, C. (1980). An analysis of learned helplessness: II. The processing of success. *Journal of Personality and Social Psychology, 39*, 940-952.

Dweck, C., & Bempechat, J., (1983). Children's theories of intelligence: Consequences for learning. In S. Paris, G. Olsen, and H. Stevenson (Eds.), *Learning and motivation in the classroom* (pp. 239–256). Hillsdale, NJ: Erlbaum.

Dweck, C., Davidson, W., Nelson, S., & Enna, B. (1978). Sex differences in learned helplessness: II. The contingencies of evaluative feedback in the classroom and III. An experimental analysis. *Developmental Psychology, 14*, 268-276.

Eccles, J. (1983). Expectancies, values, and academic behaviors. In J. Spence (Ed.), *Achievement and achievement motives: Psychological and social approaches* (pp. 75–146). New York: Freeman.

Edwards, O. (1976). Components of academic success: A profile of achieving black adolescents. *Journal of Negro Education, 45*, 408–422.

Elkind, D. (1988). *The hurried child: Growing up too fast too soon*. Reading, MA: Addison-Wesley.

Elkind, D. (1994). *Ties that stress: The new family imbalance*. Cambridge, MA: Harvard University Press.

Entwisle, D., & Hayduk, L. (1988). Lasting effects of elementary school. *Sociology of Education, 61*, 89–111.

Epstein, J. (1987). Toward a theory of family-school connections: Teacher practices and parent involvement. In K. Hurrelmann, F. Kaufmann, & F. Losel (Eds.), *Social intervention: Potential and constraints*. Hawthorne, NY: Aldine de Gruyter.

Fisher, C., Jackson, J., & Villarruel, F. (1998). The study of African American and Latin American children and youth. In W. Damon, (Series Editor), R. Lerner (Volume Editor), *Handbook of Child Psychology, Vol. II, 5th Edition* (pp. 1145–1207). New York: Wiley.

Fordham, S., & Ogbu, J. (1986). Black students' school success: Coping with the burden of acting white. *Urban Review, 18,* 176–206.

Fullilove, R. & Treisman, U. (1990). Mathematics achievement among African American undergraduates at the University of California, Berkeley: An evaluation of the Mathematics Workshop Program. *Journal of Negro Education, 59,* 463–478 .

Gamoran, A. (1988). The stratification of high school learning opportunities. *Sociology of Education, 60,* 135–155.

Gardner, H. (1983). The development of competence in culturally defined domains: A preliminary framework. In R. Shweder & R. LeVine (Eds.), *Culture theory: Essays on mind, self, and emotion* (pp. 257–275). NY: Cambridge University Press.

Garmezy, N. (1993). Children in poverty: Resilience despite risk. *Psychiatry: Interpersonal and Biological Processes, 56,* 127–136.

Garmezy, N. & Masten, A. (1990). The adaptation of children to a stressful world: Mastery of fear. In L.E. Arnold (Ed.), *Childhood stress* (pp. 459–473). New York: Wiley.

Garmezy, N. & Neuchterlein, K. (1972). Invulnerable children: The fact and fiction of competence and disadvantage. *American Journal of Orthopsychiatry, 42,* 328–329.

Ginsburg, H. (1972). *The myth of the deprived child: Poor children's intellect and education.* Upper Saddle River, NJ: Prentice Hall.

Ginsburg, H. (1986). The myth of the deprived child: New thoughts on poor children. In U. Neisser (Ed.), *The school achievement of minority children: New perspectives* (pp. 169–189). Hillsdale, NJ: Erlbaum.

Ginsburg, H. (1997). Mathematics learning disabilities: A view from developmental psychology. *Journal of Learning Disabilities, 30,* 20–33.

Ginsburg, H., Bempechat, J., & Chung, E. (1992). Parent influences on children's mathematics. In T. Sticht, M. Beeler, & B. McDonald (Eds.), *The intergenerational transfer of cognitive skills,* Vol. 2, pp. 91–121. Norwood, NJ: Ablex.

Giordano, G. (1993). The NCTM standards: A consideration of the benefits. *Race: Remedial and Special Education, 14,* 28–32.

Glazer, N., & Moynihan, D. (1963). *Beyond the melting pot: The Negroes, Puerto Ricans, Jews, Italians, and Irish of New York City.* Cambridge, MA: MIT Press.

Graham, S. (1994). Motivation in African-Americans. *Review of Educational Research, 64,* 55–117.

Graham, S. & Barker, G. (1990). The down side of help: An attributional-developmental analysis of helping behavior as a low-ability cue. *Journal of Educational Psychology, 82,* 7–15.

Greenfield, P. (1994). Independence and interdependence as developmental scripts: Implications for theory, research, and practice. In P. Greenfield & R. Cocking (Eds.), *Cross-cultural roots of minority child development* (pp. 1–37). Hillsdale, NJ: Erlbaum.

Grolnick, W. (1994). Parents' involvement in children's schooling: A multidimensional conceptualization and motivational model. *Child Development, 65,* 237–252.

Groome, T. (1998). *Educating for life: A spiritual vision for every child and parent.* Allen, TX: Thomas More.

Haggard, E. (1957). Socialization, personality, and academic achievement in gifted children. *School Review, 65,* 388–414.

Harrington, C., & Boardman, S. (1997). *Paths to success: Beating the odds in American society.* Cambridge, MA: Harvard University Press.

Haste, H. (1987). Growing into rules. In J. Bruner & H. Haste (Eds.), *Making sense: The child's construction of the world* (pp. 163–195). London: Methuen.

Haste, H. (1993). *The sexual metaphor.* Cambridge, MA: Harvard University Press.

Hatano, G. (1988). Social and motivational bases for mathematical understanding. In G. Saxe & M. Gearhart (Eds.), *Children's mathematics,* pp. 55–70. New Directions for Child Development, no. 41. San Francisco: Jossey-Bass.

Hess, R. (1991). Cultural support for schooling: Contrasts between Japan and the United States. *Educational Researcher, 20,* 2–8.

Hess, R., & Shipman, V. (1965). Early experience and the socialization of cognitive modes in children. *Child Development, 36,* 869–886.

Hess, R. D., Chang, C., & McDevitt, T. M. (1987). Cultural variations in family beliefs about children's performance in mathematics: Comparisons among People's Republic of China, Chinese-American, and Caucasian-American families. *Journal of Educational Psychology, 79,* 179–188.

Hill, P., Pierce, L., & Guthrie, J. (1990). *Reinventing public education: How contracting can transform America's schools.* Chicago: University of Chicago Press.

Hilton, T., Hsia, J., Solorzano, D., & Benton, N. (1989). *Persistence in science of high ability minority students.* Princeton, NJ: Educational Testing Service.

Ho, D. (1994). Cognitive socialization in Confucian heritage cultures. In P. Greenfield & R. Cocking (Eds.), *Cross-cultural roots of minority child development* (pp. 285–313). Hillsdale, NJ: Erlbaum.

Holloway, S. (1988). Concepts of ability and effort in Japan and the United States. *Review of Educational Research, 58,* 327–345.

Holloway, S., Gorman, K., & Fuller, B. (1988). Child rearing beliefs within diverse social structures: Mothers and daycare providers in Mexico. *International Journal of Psychology, 23,* 303–317.

Howard, J. (1995). You can't get there from here: The need for a new logic in education reform. *Daedalus, 124,* 85–92.

Irvine, J. (1996). Lessons learned: Implications for the education of African-Americans in public schools. In J. Irvine and M. Foster (Eds.), *Growing up African-American in Catholic schools* (pp. 95–105). New York: Teachers College Press.

Jimenez, N. (1998). *Ethnicity and academic achievement in adolescents of Mexican descent.* Qualifying paper, Harvard Graduate School of Education.

Kagan, J. (1989). *Unstable ideas: Temperament, cognition, and self.* Cambridge, MA: Harvard University Press.

Kao, G., & Tienda, M. (1995). Optimism and achievement: The educational performance of immigrant youth. *Social Science Quarterly, 76,* 1–19.

Keith, T., & Page, E. (1985). Do Catholic schools improve minority student achievement? *American Educational Research Journal, 22,* 337–349.

Kimchi, J. & Schaffner, B. (1990). Childhood protective factors and stress risk. In L.E. Arnold (Ed.), *Childhood stress* (pp. 475–500). New York: Wiley.

Lampert, M. (1990). When the problem is not the question and the solution is not the answer: Mathematical knowing and teaching. *American Educational Research Journal, 27,* 29–63.

Lareau, A. (1987). Social class differences in family-school relationships: The importance of cultural capital. *Sociology of Education, 60,* 73–85.

Lareau, A. (1989). *Home advantage: Social class and parental intervention in elementary education.* Philadelphia: Falmer Press.

Lee, C. (1987, April). *China's integrated approach to child care and socialization.* Invited address presented at the biennial conference of the Society for Research in Child Development, Baltimore.

Lee, V., & Bryk, A. (1988). Curriculum tracking as mediating the social distribution of high school achievement. *Sociology of Education, 61,* 78–94.

Levine, A., & Nidiffer, J. (1995). *Beating the odds: How the poor get to college.* San Francisco: Jossey-Bass.

LeVine, R. (1977). Child rearing as cultural adaptation. In P. Leiderman, S. Tulkin, & A. Rosenfeld (Eds.), *Culture and infancy: Variations in the human experience* (pp. 15–27). New York: Academic Press.

Lewis, M. (1995). The nature of cause, the role of antecedent conditions in children's attribution, and emotional behavior. *Psychological Inquiry, 6,* 305–307.

Liu, E. (1998). *The accidental Asian.* New York: Random House.

Livengood, J. (1992). Students' motivational goals and beliefs about effort and ability as they relate to college academic success. *Research in Higher Education, 33,* 247–261.

Luster, T. & McAdoo, H. (1994). Factors related to the achievement and adjustment of young African American children. *Child Development, 65,* 1080–1094.

Marsh, H. (1984). Relations among dimensions of self-attribution, dimensions of self-concept, and academic achievement. *Journal of Educational Psychology, 76,* 1291–1308.

Marsh, H. (1991, May). Public, Catholic single-sex, and Catholic coeducational high schools: Their effect on achievement, affect, and behaviors. *American Journal of Education,* 320–356.

Marsh, H., Cairns, L., Relich, J., Barnes, J., & Debus, R. (1984). The relationship between dimensions of self-attribution and dimensions of self-concept. *Journal of Educational Psychology, 76,* 3–32.

Martin, J. (1992). *The homeschool.* Cambridge, MA: Harvard University Press.

Matute-Bianchi, M. (1991). Situational ethnicity and patterns of school performance among immigrant and non-immigrant Mexican-descent students. In M. Gibson & J. Ogbu (Eds.), *Minority status and schooling* (pp. 205–247). New York: Garland.

Mordkowitz, E., & Ginsburg, H. (1987). Early academic socialization of successful Asian-American college students. *Quarterly Newsletter of the Laboratory for Comparative Human Cognition, 9,* 85–91.

Mullis, I., & Jenkins, L. (1988). *The science report card: Elements of risk and recovery.* Princeton, NJ: Educational Testing Service.

Nakkula, M. & Ravitch, S. (1998). *Matters of interpretation: Reciprocal transformation in therapeutic and developmental relationships with youth.* San Francisco: Jossey-Bass.

National Educational Goals Panel (1995). *The core report.* Washington, DC: Author.

National Mathematics Education Board (1993). *Measuring up: Prototypes for mathematics assessment.* Washington, DC: National Academy Press.

Newman, R., & Stevenson, H. (1990). Children's achievement and causal attributions in mathematics and reading. *Journal of Experimental Education, 58,* 197–212.

Nicholls, J. (1978). The development of the conceptions of effort and ability, perception of academic attainment, and the understanding that difficult tasks require more ability. *Child Development, 49,* 800–814.

Nicholls, J. (1989). *The competitive ethos and democratic education.* Cambridge, MA: Harvard University Press.

Nicholls, J. (1990). What is ability and why are we mindful of it? A developmental perspective. In R. Sternberg & J. Kolligian (Eds.), *Competence considered* (pp. 11–40). New Haven, CT: Yale University Press.

Oakes, J. (1985). *Keeping track*. Cambridge, MA: Harvard University Press.

Ogbu, J. (1986). The consequences of the American caste system. In U. Neisser (Ed.), *The school achievement of minority children*. Hillsdale, NJ: Erlbaum.

Ogbu, J. (1990). Literacy and schooling in subordinate cultures: The case of Black Americans. In K. Lomotey (Ed.), *Going to school: The African American experience* (pp. 113–131). Albany, NY: SUNY Press.

Ogbu, J. (1995). *Community forces and minority educational strategies: A comparative study. Final report #1: Student survey*. Unpublished manuscript, University of California, Berkeley.

Pallas, A., Natriello, G., & McDill, E. (1989). The changing nature of the disadvantaged population: Current dimensions and future trends. *Educational Researcher, 18*, 16–22.

Parsons, J., Adler, T., & Kaczala, C. (1982). Socialization of achievement attitudes and beliefs: Parental influences. *Child Development, 53*, 310–321.

Peng, S., & Wright, D. (1994). Explanation of academic achievement of Asian American students. *Journal of Educational Research, 87*, 346–352.

Phillips, D. (1987). Socialization of perceived academic competence among highly competent children. *Child Development, 58*, 1308–1320.

Piaget, Jean (1926). *The language and thought of the child*. New York: Harcourt Brace.

Piaget, J. (1963). *The origins of intelligence in children*. New York: Norton.

Polite, V. (1996). Making a way out of no way: The Oblate sisters of Providence and St. Francis Academy in Baltimore, Maryland, 1828–present. In J. Irvine and M. Foster (Eds.), *Growing up African-American in Catholic schools* (pp. 62–75). New York: Teachers College Press.

Quihuis, G. & Bempechat, J. (1997, April). Identifying students' implicit theories of intelligence: A survey and interview study. Poster presented at the Biennial Conference of the Society for Research in Child Development, Washington, DC.

Quihuis, G., Bempechat, J. & Jimenez, N. (1998, April). Implicit theories of intelligence across academic domains: A study of meaning making in context. Poster presented at the Annual Conference of the American Educational Research Association, San Diego.

Reese, L., Balzano, S., Gallimore, R., & Goldenberg, C. (in press). *The concept of "educaciòn": Latino family values and American schooling*.

Resnick, L. (1995). Education reform: What's not being said. *Daedalus, 124*, 55–62.

Rogoff, B. (1990). *Apprenticeship in thinking: Cognitive development in a social context*. New York: Oxford University Press.

Rogoff, B., & Chavajay, P. (1995). What's become of research on the cultural basis of cognitive development? *American Psychologist, 50*, 859–877.

Rogoff, B., & Gardner, W. (1984). Adult guidance of everyday cognition. In B. Rogoff & J. Lave (Eds.). *Everyday cognition: Its development in social context*. Cambridge, MA: Harvard University Press.

Rosen, B., & D'Andrade, R. (1959). The psychosocial origins of achievement motivation. *Sociometry, 22*, 185–218.

Rosenthal, R. (1995). Critiquing Pygmalion: A twenty-five year perspective. *Current Directions in Psychological Science, 4*, 169–171.

Rosenthal, R., & Jacobson, L. (1968). *Pygmalion in the classroom: Teacher expectation and pupils' intellectual development*. Austin, TX: Holt, Rinehart and Winston.

Ruthven, K. (1994). Better judgement: Rethinking assessment in mathematics education. *Educational Studies in Mathematics, 27*, 433–450.

Rutter, M. (1987). Psychosocial resilience and protective mechanisms. *American Journal of Orthopsychiatry, 57*, 316–331.

Schiller, D., & Walberg, H. (1982). Japan: The learning society. *Educational Leadership, 40*, 14–16.

Schneider, B., Hieshima, J., Lee, S., & Plank, S. (1994). East-Asian academic success in the United States: Family, school, and community expectations. In P. Greenfield and R. Cocking (Eds.), *Cross-cultural roots of minority child development* (pp. 323–350). Hillsdale, NJ: Erlbaum.

Schunk, D. (1995). Implicit theories and achievement behavior. *Psychological Inquiry, 6*, 311–314.

Schurmans, M., & Dasen, P. (1992). Social representations of intelligence: Cote d'Ivoire and Switzerland. In M. von Cranach, W. Doise, & G. Mugny (Eds.), *Social representations and the social bases of knowledge* (pp. 144–152). Lewiston, NY: Hogrefe & Huber.

Schwartz, J. (1995). Shuttling between the particular and the general: Reflections on the role of conjecture and hypothesis in the generation of knowledge in science and mathematics. In D. Perkins & J. Schwartz (Eds.), *Software goes to school: Teaching for understanding with new technologies* (pp. 93–105). New York: Oxford University Press.

Scott-Jones, D. (1987). Mother as teacher in the families of high- and low-achieving low-income first graders. *Journal of Negro Education*, 21–34.

Shields, P. (1996). Holy angels: Pocket of excellence. In J. Irvine and M. Foster (Eds.), *Growing up African-American in Catholic schools* (pp. 76–84). New York: Teachers College Press.

Shweder, R. (1990). Cultural psychology—what is it? In J. Stigler, R. Shweder, & G. Herdt (Eds.), *Cultural psychology: Essays on comparative human development* (pp. 1–43). New York: Cambridge University Press.

Shweder, R. (1991). *Thinking through cultures: Expeditions in cultural psychology.* Cambridge, MA: Harvard University Press.

Sigel, I. (1985). A conceptual analysis of beliefs. In I. Sigel (Ed.), *Parental belief systems* (pp. 345–371). Hillsdale, NJ: Erlbaum.

Sigel, I. (1992). Introduction. In J. Roopnarine & D. B. Carter (Eds.), *Annual advances in applied developmental psychology: Vol. 5. Parent-child socialization in diverse cultures* (pp. ix-x). Norwood, NJ: Ablex.

Sigel, I., McGillicuddy-DeLisi, A., & Goodnow, J. (1992). Introduction to the second edition. In I. Sigel, A. McGillicuddy-DeLisi, & J. Goodnow (Eds.), *Parental belief systems: The psychological consequences for children* 2nd ed., (pp. xiii-xv). Hillsdale, NJ: Erlbaum.

Slaughter-Defoe, D., Nakagawa, K., Takanashi, R., & Johnson, D. (1990). Toward cultural/ecological perspectives on schooling and achievement in African and Asian-American children. *Child Development, 61.*

Snow, C., Barnes, W., Chandler, B., Goodman, I., & Hemphill, L. (1991). *Unfulfilled expectations: Home and school influences on literacy.* Cambridge, MA: Harvard University Press.

Steinberg, L., Dornbusch, S., & Brown, B. (1992). Ethnic differences in adolescent achievement: An ecological perspective. *American Psychologist, 47,* 723–729.

Stevenson, H. (1993). Why Asian students still outdistance Americans. *Educational Leadership, 50,* 63–65.

Stevenson, H., Chen, C., & Lee, S. (1993). Mathematics achievement of Chinese, Japanese, and American children: Ten years later. *Science, 259,* 53–58.

Stevenson, H., Lee, S., & Stigler, J. (1986). Mathematics achievement of Chinese, Japanese and American children. *Science, 231,* 693–699.

Stevenson, H., & Stigler, J. (1992). *The learning gap.* New York: Summit Books.

Stigler, J. W., & Perry, M. (1990). Mathematics learning in Japanese, Chinese, and American classrooms. In J. W. Stigler, R. A. Shweder, & G. Herdt (Eds.), *Cultural psychology: Essays on comparative human development* (pp. 328–353). New York: Cambridge University Press.

Stipek, D. J., & Gralinski, J. H. (1991). Gender differences in children's achievement-related beliefs and emotional responses to success and failure in mathematics. *Journal of Educational Psychology, 83,* 361–371.

Suarez-Orozco, C., & Suarez-Orozco, M. (1995). *Transformations: Migration, family life, and achievement motivation among Latino adolescents.* Palo Alto, CA: Stanford University Press.

Sue, S., & Okazaki, S. (1990). Asian American educational achievements: A phenomenon in search of an explanation. *American Psychologist, 45,* 913–920.

Suskind, R. (1998). *A hope in the unseen: An American odyssey from the inner city to the Ivy league*. New York: Broadway Books.

Toby, J. (1957). Orientation to education as a factor in the school maladjustment of lower class children. *Social Forces, 38*, 259–266.

U.S. Department of Education (1998). *The educational system in Japan: Case study findings*. Washington, DC: Office of Educational Research and Improvement.

Valenzuela, A., & Dornbusch, S. (1994). Familism and social capital in the academic achievement of Mexican-origin and Anglo adolescents. *Social Science Quarterly, 75*, 18–36.

Vygotsky, L. (1962). *Thought and language*. (E. Hanfman & G. Bakar, Eds. and Trans.). Cambridge, MA: MIT Press.

Vygotsky, L. (1978). *Mind in society*. (M. Cole, V. John-Steiner, S. Scribner, & E. Souberman, Eds.). Cambridge, MA: Harvard University Press.

Weiner, B. (1985). Principles for a theory of student motivation and their application within an attributional framework. In R. Ames and C. Ames (Eds.), *Research on motivation in education*. Vol. 1, *Student motivation*. New York: Academic Press.

Weiner, B. (1994). Integrating social and personal theories of achievement strivings. *Review of Educational Research, 64*, 557–573.

Weiner, B., Graham, S., Stern, P., & Lawson, M. (1982). Using affective cues to infer causal thoughts. *Developmental Psychology, 21*, 102–107.

Werner, E., & Smith, R. (1989). *Vulnerable but invincible: A longitudinal study of resilient children and youth*. New York: McGraw-Hill.

White, M. (1987). *The Japanese educational challenge*. New York: Free Press.

White, M., & LeVine, R. (1987). What is an "ii ko" (good child)? In H. Stevenson, H. Azuma, & K. Hakuta (Eds.), *Child development and education in Japan* (pp. 55–62). New York: Freeman.

Wu, J. (1992). *The relationship between ethnic identity and achievement motivation in Chinese Americans and Filipino Americans*. Unpublished dissertation, Harvard University.

York, D. (1996). The academic achievement of African-Americans in Catholic schools: A review of the literature. In J. Irvine and M. Foster (Eds.), *Growing up African-American in Catholic schools* (pp. 11–46). New York: Teachers College Press.

About the Author

Janine Bempechat is assistant professor of education at the Harvard Graduate School of Education, where she received her Ed.D. degree in Human Development and Psychology. Bempechat is a past National Academy of Education Spencer Fellow. Her research on achievement and motivation in poor and minority children has been supported by the Spencer Foundation and the National Science Foundation. She lives in Newton, Massachusetts with her husband and two children

Index

. . . .

A

Ability: achievement and belief in, 30–31, 32, 80, 81–82, 93; activating one's, 61, 97–98; age and beliefs about, 24–25, 58; beliefs in cooperative classrooms, 97–98; blaming failure on lack of, 81–82, 91, 97; children's meaning making about, 126; children's perceptions of, 22–25, 38, 98, 110; cultural views of effort and, 58–61, 62–65, 114; effort and presence of, 59–60, 68, 82, 114; experiment on manipulating beliefs about, 118; as innate, fixed, and limited capacity, 21, 22, 25, 61, 81–82, 97, 114; as mastery through effort, 25, 59–60; and mathematics achievement, 38–39, 80–82; self-perception of effort and, 38, 84, 111; tracking by, 58, 92. *See also* Success and failure, children's understanding of

"Ability" model of learning, 95

Abrahams, S., 126–127

Academic achievement. *See* Achievement

Academic curricula: Catholic schools focus on, 55, 58, 92; mathematics education, 75–76; spiraling or brand new yearly, 72; and tracking, 58, 92

Academic support: and achievement in mathematics, 79–80, 82–83; by parents, 26, 34, 83, 140; children's perceptions of, 45–47; findings on, 45–47; as not absolutely necessary, 39–40; research on, 34–37, 39, 79–80. *See also* Parental involvement

Achievement: and causality issues, 26–27, 30–31, 67; higher in Catholic schools, 26, 32; home-school-community partnership for, 16, 111–112, 112–113; measures of, 26; psychological obstacles to, 133–134. *See also* Effort and school achievement; Success in school, overall

Achievement beliefs: of adolescents growing up under apartheid, 129, 130–135; Asian culture, 48–49; of black children, 127–128; children's reasons and, 21–22; and cognitive socialization, 46, 90; findings on, 80–82; and outcomes, 30–32, 89–91; studied in context, 129–135; studying children's, 10–11, 21–22, 29–30. *See also* Success and failure, children's understanding of; Underachievement

Achievement in mathematics, 69–84; American student record of problems with, 69–70; Asian "effort"